Guitar in Theory and Practice

Art Director and Layout Design: Jeff Napadow

Copyright © 2011 Kevin M Buck

Eternal Eye Publishing

All rights reserved. No part of this book may be reproduced or transmitted in any form, electronic or mechanical, including photocopying, or by any information storage or retrieval system, without written permission of the author.

Library of Congress Control Number: 2011934211

ISBN: 0983534705

ISBN-13: 9780983534709

Acknowledgement

I have learned so much about music from so many places. I cannot tell you exactly where I learned some of this info, or from where it all originated. Some of these ideas are recurring thought forms that have been around forever. I discovered much of this by trial and error, and by personal reflection and study. However, I still must give an incomplete list of people who I have learned from, either directly or indirectly. I recommend looking into all of their work, as well as all of my work, for future study. They have all helped me to learn and develop many of the ideas in this book through their words, writing, or by analysis of their compositions, philosophies, playing styles and music. I also owe thanks to every book, magazine, television program, and conversation that I ever had with anyone about music.

Uli Jon Roth, Harry Hmura, Joe Satriani, Steve Vai, Randy Rhoads, Ritchie Blackmore, Yngwie J. Malmsteen, Jason Becker, Marty Friedman, Jimi Hendrix, Allan Holdsworth, Al Di Meola, Johann Sebastian Bach, Wolfgang Amadeus Mozart, Ludwig Van Beethoven, Niccolo Paganini, Claude Debussy, Arnold Schoenberg, John Coltrane, Django Reinhard, Pythagorus, Aleister Crowley. . . and thousands of other people that I cannot remember, but to whom I owe much for their infinite wisdom.

I also should acknowledge the fact that without the support from my loving wife Laura, her parents Leslie and Ellen Zurawic, my mom Marilyn and her husband Richard Dort, my dad Ronald E. Buck, Jeff Napadow, and so many of my friends. I certainly would not have been able to create this book, or any of my musick for that matter, without you. I am eternally grateful for the sacrifices you have all made, and continue to make for me, to live my dream of being a full-time musician. This book is a product of all of your dedication.

TABLE OF CONTENTS

- Introduction — 3
- What to Learn in order — 4
- Names of the Strings — 5
- Note Names — 6
- Chords (Open, Bar and Seventh) — 7
- Scales — 15
- Major Scale and the Modes — 17
- Pentatonic Scale Fingerings — 19
- Mode Fingerings (As Six Note Shapes) — 21
- Mode Fingerings (As Three Notes Per String in A Major) — 24
- One Octave Scale Fingerings — 27
- Diagonal Shapes Using Octaves — 31
- Mode Fingerings (in A Minor, A Harmonic, A Melodic, and A Hungarian Minor as Three Note Per String Fingerings) — 32
- Conventional Mode Fingerings — 40
- Arpeggios (Three, Four, Five, and Six String Fingerings for Major, Minor, Diminished and Augmented) — 43
- Seventh Arpeggios (Three, Five, and Six String Fingerings for Major 7th, Dominant 7th, Minor 7th, ½ Diminished and Diminished 7th) — 52
- Chords, Arpeggios, and Seventh Chords — 63
- Diff'rent Strokes Alternate Picking Licks — 68
- Licks, Sequences, Runs — 70
- Rhythm — 78
- Chord Scales — 85
- How to Find the Key of Riffs — 87
- Formulas for Chords, Arpeggios, and Scales — 90
- Transcendental Wisdom — 93
- Extras — 96

Introduction

I created this book to give guitar players a method to become better musicians by taking the most important ideas of music and presenting them in a simplistic way for guitar players. *Guitar in Theory and Practice* is a systematic guide to learning all of the scales, chords and arpeggios needed for improvisation. This book includes the only proven method to learning how to play and memorize seventh arpeggios with fingerings and examples. It is designed to help students learn, memorize, and play scales, chords and arpeggios in a new way so that they can play and create the music that they always wanted to. This book also gives examples of the difficult techniques that need to be practiced on the guitar in order to become a proficient soloist. *Guitar in Theory and Practice* teaches students how to create their own music, and how to use these various scales, chords and arpeggios in their soloing and songwriting. I also have included blank fingerboard maps, blank chord charts, blank notation sheets, blank tabulature sheets, and blank sheets with both tab and notation for you, as I have always had trouble finding them.

This book was created to show the relationships of all things, in order to help us develop our personalities and become better artists and better human beings. It also provides insights to gain a greater understanding of music and life (as music and art are a reflection of life). *Guitar in Theory and Practice* is the first book containing a poster that relates astrological signs, pitches, colors, planets, gods, elements of life, masculine and feminine dualities, time, intervals, numbers, modes and chakras. If you learn anything of value from this book, please share it with others, because music is meant to be shared and should always evolve.

What to learn in order

Many guitar players I know have trouble remembering all the various things that they learn. They learn certain things, but cannot relate them to everything else. They have a bunch of information (chords, scales, licks, songs, riffs, etc.) just floating around in their heads, and they end up chasing their tails - learning new things while forgetting the things they had previously learned. You can use this as a guide to what you should learn and memorize.

Think of music or guitar as a tree, and all the aspects/elements of music are branches on that tree. By organizing the individual chords/arpeggios (arpeggios are just chords with the notes played individually) and scales properly we can quickly identify the information in our mind like a filing cabinet system. For the most part, all music can be identified by chords and scales, also known as harmony and melody, or riffs and solos.

Of course, this tree branch approach can work with any element of music, such as rhythm, memorizing songs, dynamics, technique, timbre, form, etc. You must be sure you memorize the first thing before going to the second, then be sure you have the first and second things memorized before moving on to the third. Then, eventually the tree will be huge and healthy. Otherwise you will be juggling too much information, and it will be difficult to get anywhere.

Outside of obvious practices like working on technique, rhythm, reading, writing, learning songs, improvising, jamming, recording, transcribing, creating songs and watching sports on TV, you must also learn (and memorize) scales and chords. The following pages contain a systematic approach to which chords/arpeggios and which scales we should learn (and memorize) in a general order of importance. Depending on the genre of music you play, the order of importance will change.

Names of the Strings

The string closest to the ground (highest in pitch) is known as your 1st string.

Your 1st string is also known as the high E string.

The one above that is your 2nd string and is also known as your B string.

The one above that is your 3rd string and is also known as your G string.

The one above that is your 4th string and is also known as your D string.

The one above that is your 5th string and is also known as your A string.

The one above that is your 6th string and is also known as your low E string.

If you are a beginner or teaching a beginner you can use the mnemonic

Every   **B**oy   **G**ets   **D**runk   **A**t   **E**d's
1st   2nd   3rd   4th   5th   6th

This is an easy way to remember the names of the strings from *high to low*.
The name of the string is also the name of the pitch it produces when plucked open.

Note Names Throughout the Fingerboard

The Music Alphabet

In music we use letters for the note names. The music alphabet has only seven letters and goes ABCDEFG. After G it goes back to an A (though it is a higher version of the pitch A, which is known as an *octave* higher). **ABCDEFGABCDEFGAB...**

This goes up and down until you run out of the instrument's range or until the human ear cannot hear the highest or lowest of notes anymore. So again, A is after G, and G is before A in the musical alphabet.

Steps

In music there are things called *whole steps* and *half steps*. A whole step is basically a two fret distance, and a half step is basically a one fret distance. There are whole steps between all notes except between B and C, and between E and F. These notes only have half steps between them. So, essentially, what that means is that all the notes are two frets apart, except between B to C, and E to F. They are only one fret apart.

Sharps and Flats

A sharp symbol looks like this: ♯ and it means raise the note a half step.
A flat symbol looks like this: ♭ and it means lower the note a half step.
A note that is a half step higher than A is called A♯
A note that is a half step lower than A, would be called A♭
It is very important to be able to identify what any note is on the fingerboard quickly. The note names on the 12th fret are the same as the open strings. This is because in western music we have only twelve different notes including the sharps and flats.

After memorizing the note names in the open and twelfth positions, I recommend memorizing what they are around the fifth and eight positions because that way it will be easier and faster to memorize all of them. When tuning a guitar by ear you are basically matching pitches, so use this as a way to help you identify notes. Also, learning about octaves can help with identifying note names as well. A good exercise is to take a note name and see if you can find that note on every string. I also like the exercise of choosing a fret position on the guitar neck and seeing if you can name all of the note names from the high E string to the low E string (or from low E string to the high E string).

Chords (Open, Bar, and Seventh)

Start by memorizing power chords and the basic eight open chords
(A, Am, C, D, Dm, E, Em, and G). Notice that I went from A to G, or first to last. You may want to learn some open seventh chords as well, **(A7, B7, C7, D7, E7, and G7)** especially if you play blues or jazz. You must memorize all the basic chords/triads with three different notes in them and the inversions of those chords/triads. There are only four types of chords/triads with three different notes in them.

Major, Minor, Diminished, and Augmented

First, memorize five and six string rooted bar chord fingerings (known as basic grips). Then, try to memorize all the fingerings and inversions of these three note chords.

Then, move on to chords with four different notes in them. The first four basic chords we should learn with four different notes in them are known as diatonic seventh chords. They are also referred to as polychords because they have two different triads contained within them.

Major 7th, Minor 7th, Dominant 7th, and ½ Diminished

After memorizing the diatonic seventh chords, you should then memorize suspended and add chords. The difference between suspended and add chords is that suspended chords have no 3rd, while add chords just add another note to the chord without taking out the 3rd.

sus9, add9, sus4, add4, add♯11, sus♯11, minor add9, minor add4, and then various 6 chords and min6 chords

After memorizing the suspended and add chords you can then learn:

Minor/Major 7th, Major 7♯5, Diminished 7th

These chords work in harmonic minor keys, and various other keys and scales (diminished 7th is very common in classical and heavy metal).

Then, learn some chords with five or more notes in them. Also learn about the family of dominant seventh chords:

9th, 11th, and 13th (essential for blues and jazz)

The family of major seventh chords:

Major 9th, Major 11th, Major 13th

The family of minor seventh chords:
minor 9th, minor 11th, minor 13th

Altered seventh chords:

Dom7♭(5, Dom7♯5, Dom7♭9, Dom7♯9, Dom7♭13, Dom7♯11

The altered chords allow you to raise or lower the 9th or 5th interval, raise the 11th, flat the 13th, or any combination of them. An example of this is a **dom7♯5♭9♯11 chord**.

This, of course, is not a complete list, but a good start. You should learn about chord theory and the formulas of these chords after memorizing a certain amount of basic grip six string and five string rooted chords and their inversions. The seventh chord inversions are very good for jazz and walking bass fingerstyle blues. The four string seventh chord inversions are the same as the other seventh chord inversions, but the note on the high E string is moved to the low E string. When learning the inversions of four string seventh chords, memorize which shape comes before and after each shape, memorize where the root notes are, then figure out where the thirds, fifths and sevenths are in order to change the quality or alter these chords. Organize these chord types from first to last. Do not learn any new chords until you have memorized the last group to assure that you will not forget what you previously learned. Do this with every aspect of music you learn. Otherwise, you may end up chasing your tail and not retaining enough information to get very far.

OPEN CHORDS

D Major
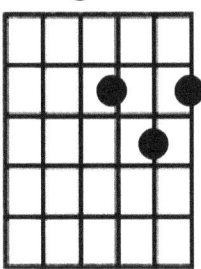

D minor
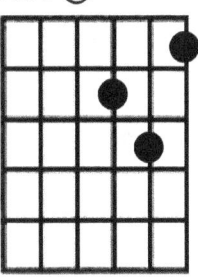

A Major
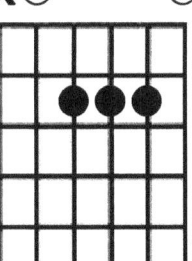

A minor
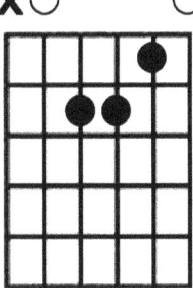

E Major
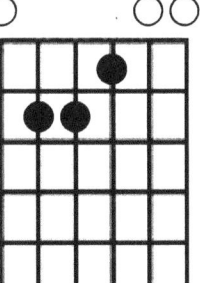

E minor
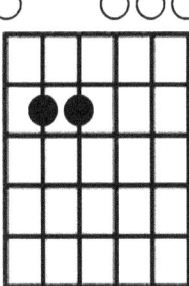

G Major
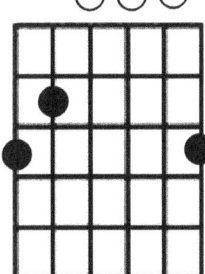

C Major
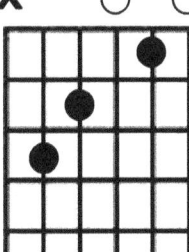

BAR CHORDS

(6 string rooted chords)   *(5 string rooted chords)*

A Major
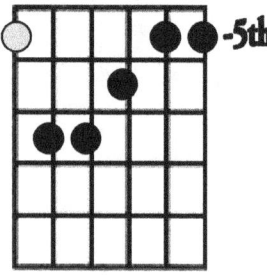

D Major
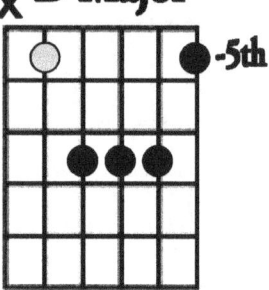

A minor
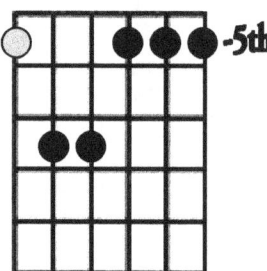

D minor
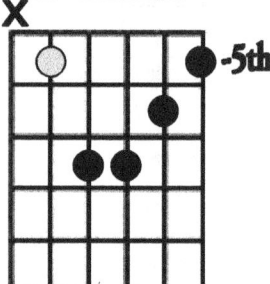

A diminished
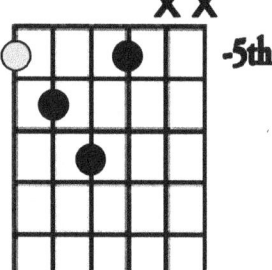

D diminished
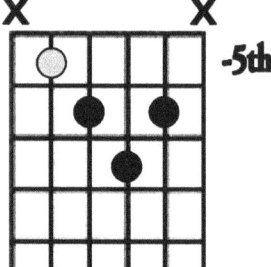

A Augmented
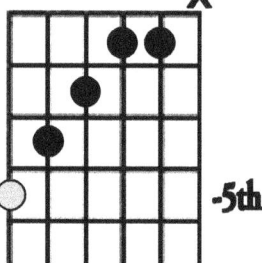

D Augmented
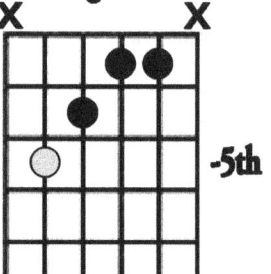

- 10 -   Chords (Open, Bar, and Seventh)

Diatonic Seventh Chords

(6 string rooted chords)   *(5 string rooted chords)*

A Major 7
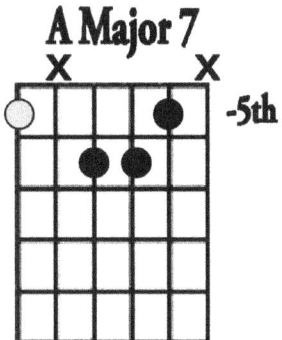

D Major 7
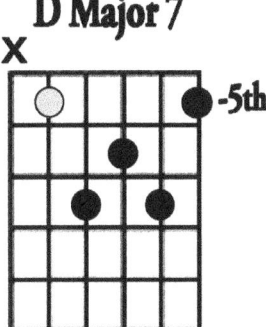

A Dominant 7
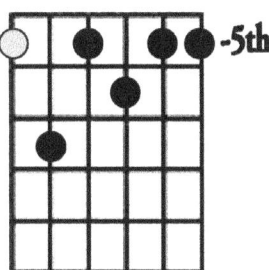

D Dominant 7
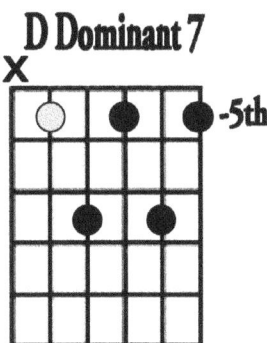

A minor 7
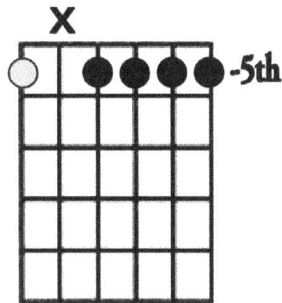

D minor 7
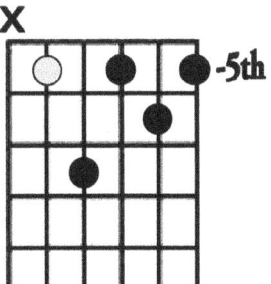

A 1/2 diminished

D 1/2 diminished
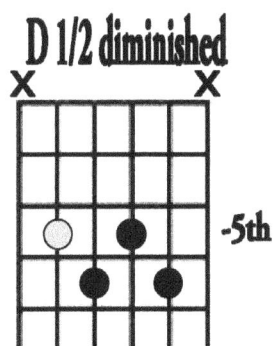

Guitar in Theory and Practice

OPEN Dominant 7th CHORDS

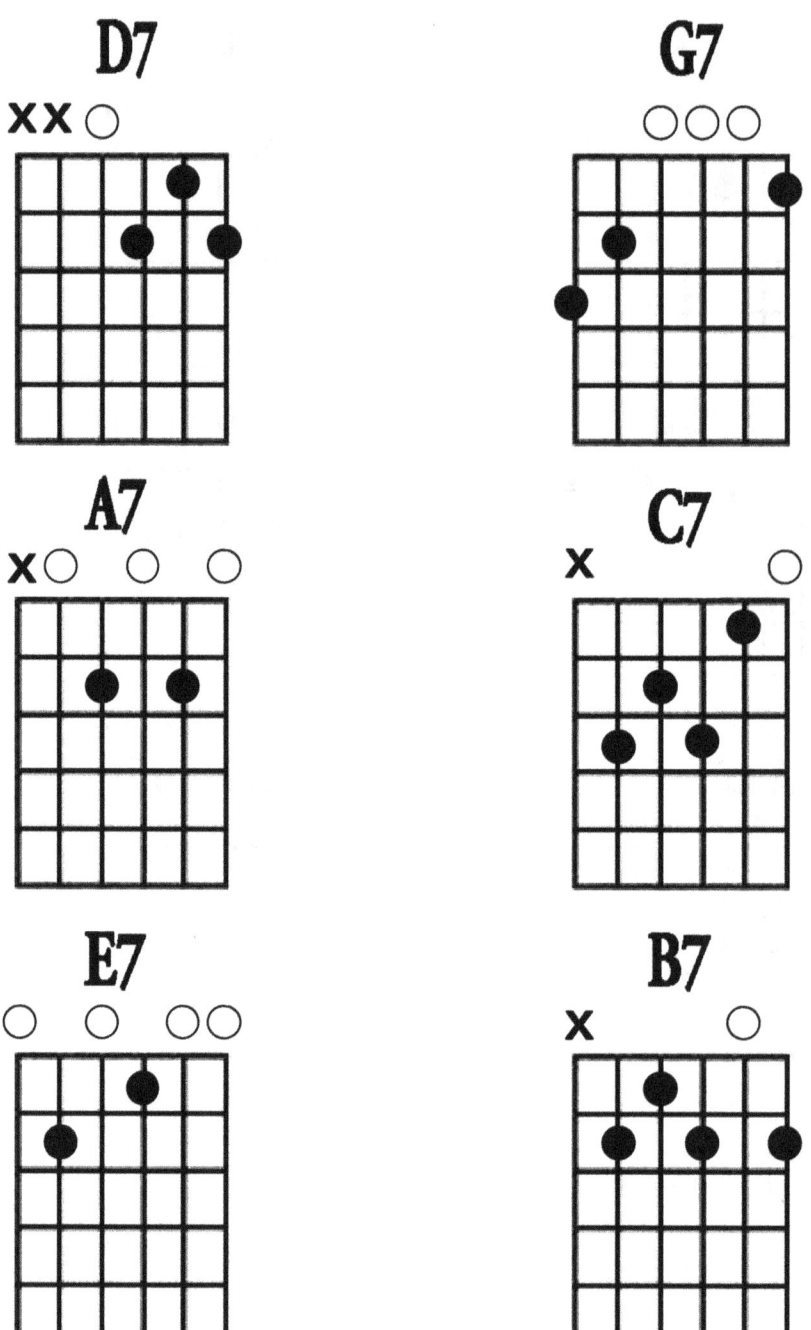

4 string Seventh Chord inversions

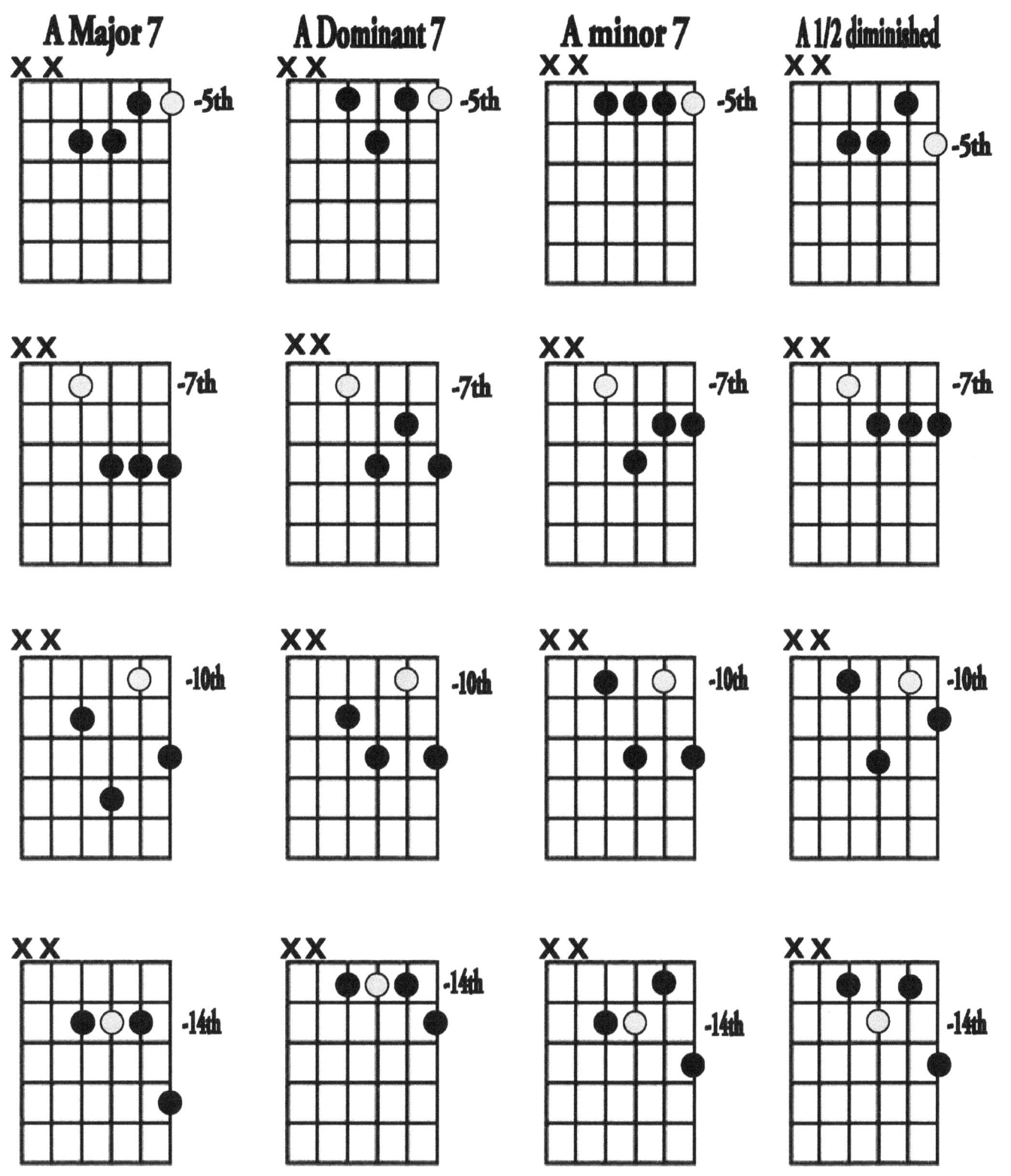

Guitar in Theory and Practice - 13 -

Seventh Chord inversions

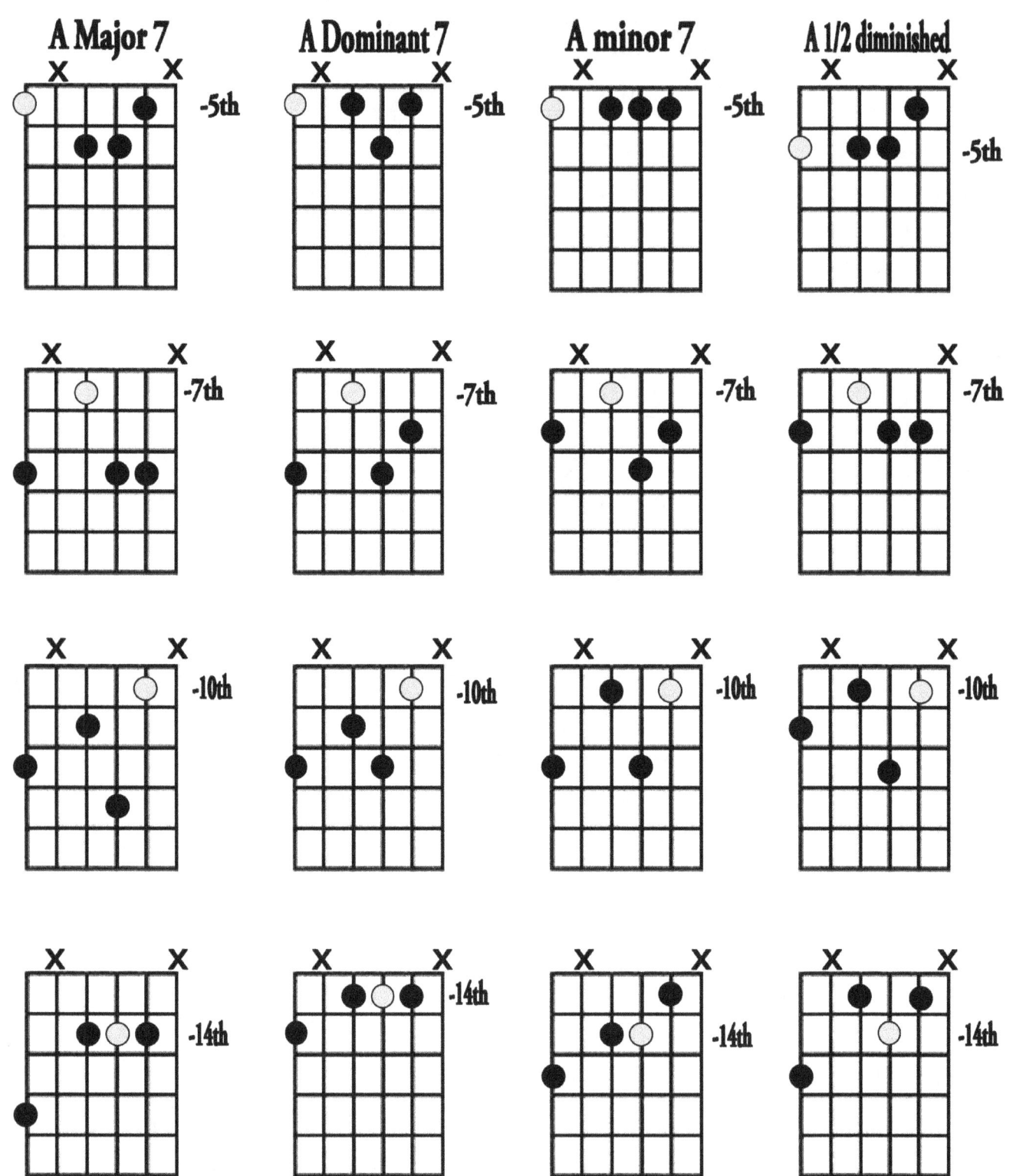

- 14 -   *Chords (Open, Bar, and Seventh)*

Scales

Here is a list of the scales that you should learn and memorize:

Major and minor pentatonic scales

Major and minor blues scales

Major and minor scales and modes (Ionian, Dorian, Phrygian, Lydian, Mixolydian, Aeolian, and Locrian)

Harmonic minor scale and modes (especially the more common Phrygian dominant mode)

Melodic minor scale and modes (especially the Lydian Dominant, and Super Locrian modes)

Hybrid blues scales (mixing all pentatonic, blues, Mixodorian and Mixodorianblues scale)

Chromatic scales

Diminished scales (the half/whole and the whole/half)

Augmented/Whole tone scales

Hungarian minor scales and modes

Gypsy minor scales and modes

Harmonic major scales and modes

Then learn several other types of **pentatonic, hexatonic, diatonic, exotic, altered, symmetrical, and/or synthetic scales.**

I personally enjoy the gypsy-like **Melodic minor with a♯4th** and all the modes in it. Also look at **a Melodic minor with a ♭2nd** and all the modes in it.

There are many other types of scales. Some even take more than one octave to complete. Many eastern scales divide the octave into more than twelve parts as well. I like the concept of creating scales by stacking different types of intervals on top of one another until you reach the starting note in some higher octave.

Make sure you dwell on the feeling that each of these chords/arpeggios and scales evoke in you when you hear them. This way, you will recognize them later when you hear them, which helps tremendously when trying to transcribe music. Perhaps meditate on their color, or think of various memories and feelings that you get when hearing them. Or, at least relate them to a melody, a song or a guitarist that uses them.

Don't feel overloaded because of the fact that there is so much to learn. Remember every long journey begins with one step, and I hope this information will help you on your journey. The best professional golfers win tournaments by taking it one shot at a time. The best poker players win tournaments by taking it one hand at a time. You, my friend, should try to learn just one chord, or one scale, or one song at a time, and not think of the vast amount of things that you could learn.

The Major Scale and the Modes

If you know a major scale, then you already can play every mode. There are seven different notes in the major scale. The eighth note is the same as the first note, but it is an octave higher.

Everything in music is based off of the major scale. We number each note of the major scale. The first note is 1, the second note is 2, the third note is 3, and so forth, we just use roman numerals (I, ii, iii, etc.).

Intervals are the distance between each note. These distances are based off the major scale. The distance between the 1st note and the 2nd note is called a second. The distance between the 1st note and the 3rd note is called a third. The distance between the 1st and 4th note is called a fourth and so on. It is very important to eventually learn about the inversions of these intervals and to memorize all twelve simple intervals by sound, shape, and feeling.

If you start on the first note of the major scale, play some stuff, and end on the first note you are in the first mode Ionian. If you start on the second note of the major scale, play some stuff, and end on the second note, then you are in the 2nd mode Dorian, even though you played it out of your major scale.

Here is an example. To sing a major scale in the solfege (do re mi fa so la ti do) would be:

If a melody starts on DO (or I) and ends on DO (or I) then you are in Ionian.

Here is an example:

Those notes in major scale are 1 2 3 4 5 3 4 2 1

If you start a melody on re (or ii) and end on re (or ii) then you are in Dorian

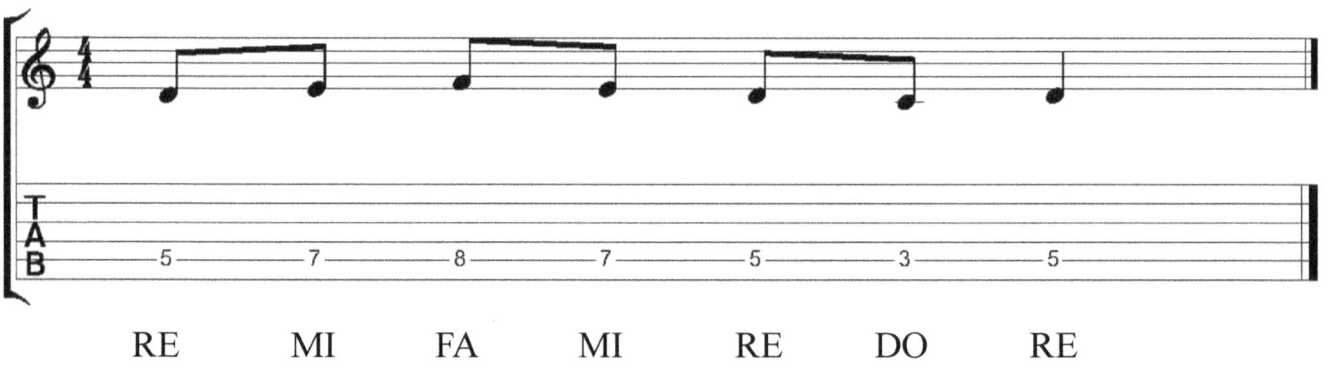

Those notes in a major scale are 2 3 4 3 2 1 2

Since the melody is based around the 2nd note of the scale, it is in Dorian because Dorian is the 2nd mode. Notice how this melody is darker then the melody in Ionian.

It is important to be able to find the first note of the major scale (1) no matter which number note that you may be on. This can be done by using major scale fingerings, using the formula in steps, or using numbers.

The major scale formula in steps is Whole, Whole, Half, Whole, Whole, Whole, Half (1,1,½,1,1,1,½). There is a half step between the 3rd and 4th notes and between the 7th and 8th notes. Knowing this will allow us to find the first scale degree by thinking of the numbers of each note of the scale.

Pentatonic Scale Fingerings

Here are five two note per string fingerings (or boxes) for an A minor (or C major) pentatonic scale. Memorize where the minor and major root notes are in every fingering. The minor root notes are highlighted in dark grey and the major root notes are highlighted in light grey. Notice that the major root note is always the note that follows the minor root note. Memorize which fingering comes before and after each fingering. Beginning students should just learn the first box and learn how to make that scale sound like music by improvising with the notes of the scale and learning several basic guitar licks.

Pentatonic Scales in A minor (C Major)
five 2 note per string fingerings (Boxes)

Mode Fingerings (As Six Note Shapes)

A good way to learn the mode fingerings is to play only the first six notes of every mode fingering (three notes per string), on the low E and A strings, and/or on the B and high E strings. This will teach you to play horizontally throughout the fingerboard quite easily in any key because the shapes are always the same for all keys. This is known as the "same stuff different frets theory." There are seven different mode fingerings, but Ionian and Mixolydian have the same six note shapes because the first six notes of Mixolydian are the same as Ionian. Mixolydian has a different seventh note. Be able to play them ascending and descending up and down the neck. It is essential to memorize each name, number and shape. It is also essential to memorize which one comes before and after each one. Then, whenever you see any one of these shapes on any set of two adjacent strings you will know where the next shape is horizontally up or down the neck.

7 Modes in A Major as 6 note shapes
3 note per string fingerings

- 22 - *Mode Fingerings (As Six Note Shapes)*

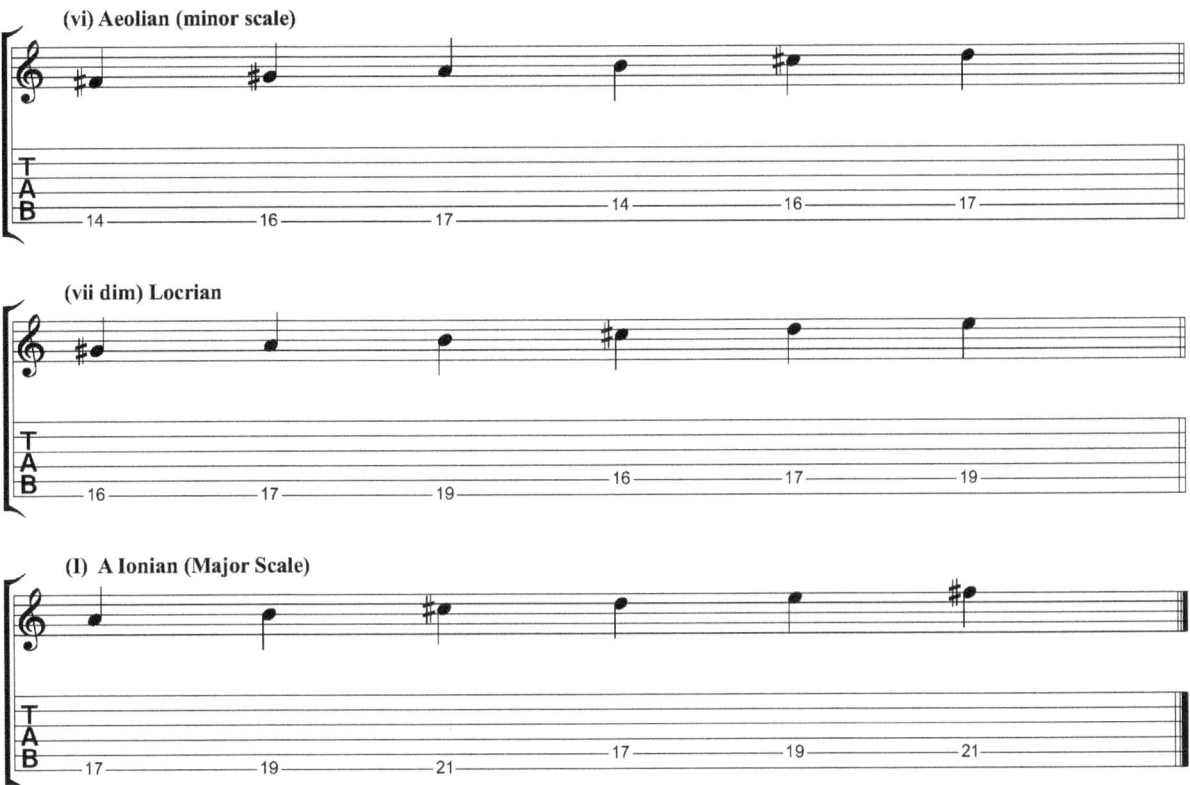

Mode Fingerings (As Three Notes Per String in A Major)
Memorizing the Modes as Three Note Per String Fingerings

If you learn the mode fingerings as six note shapes on the low E and A strings, it is very easy to memorize the fingerings for each mode on all six strings. If you know the first six notes of a mode fingering, then the next six notes will be the previous six note fingering on the next two strings in the same starting position (except for Ionian which is one position higher). Then, the next six notes will be the six note fingering previous to that one on the last two strings, but one position higher (except for Dorian which is two positions higher then you left off).

Say you start on the low E with the six notes of the Phrygian fingering, then the next six notes starting on the D string will be the previous fingering Dorian in the same position you started. Then, the next six notes starting on the B string will be the previous fingering Ionian one position higher. This method will work for minor, harmonic minor, melodic minor, and Hungarian minor scales which have all been included as three note per string fingerings. If this confuses you, just try your best to memorize the three note per string fingerings as written and look for any patterns within the fingerings.

Learn your full mode fingerings as three notes per string shapes. They are easy to memorize that way. It also makes it easier for you to figure out the patterns and shapes of the whole fingerboard in every key. I also think they are more efficient for playing really fast. Later, it will be easy to play the modes with only two notes on any one of the strings by playing two notes of the mode fingering on one string and then shifting back into the previous mode fingering to finish the scale.

7 Modes in A Major
3 note per string fingerings

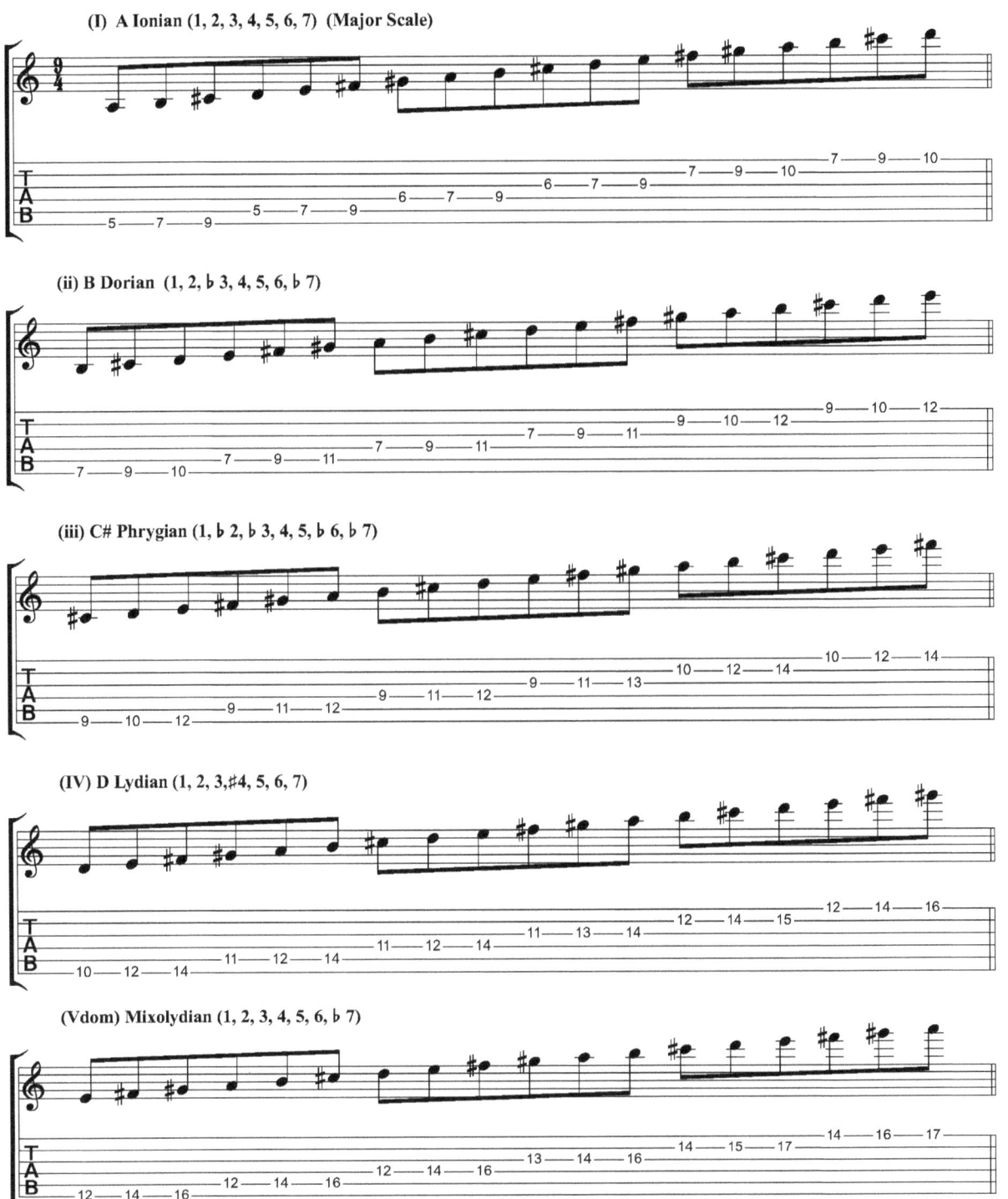

(vi) Aeolian (1, 2, ♭3, 4, 5, ♭6, ♭7) (minor scale)

(vii dim) Locrian (1, ♭2, ♭3, 4, ♭5, ♭6 ♭7)

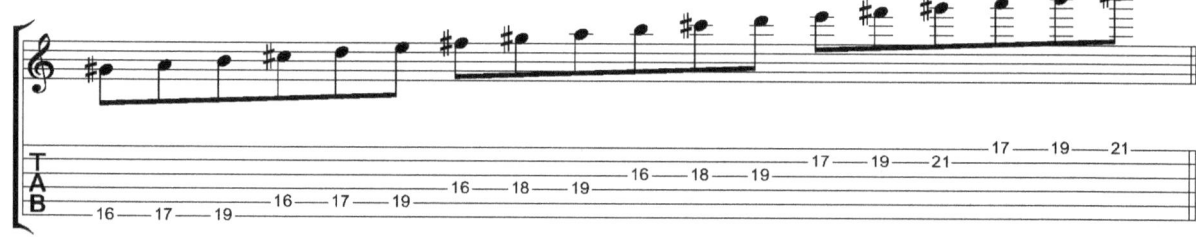

(I) A Ionian (1, 2, 3, 4, 5, 6, 7) (Major Scale)

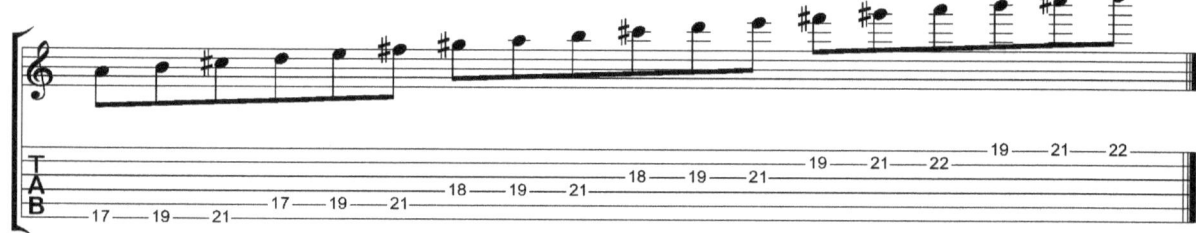

One Octave Fingerings

Playing the modes from octave to octave is also valuable, but usually is not going to help you in connecting the entire fingerboard in every key. It is important to learn how to play these scales starting with your middle, ring and pinky fingers. Learn these fingerings on different sets of strings as well.

One Octave Fingerings
for Major, Harmonic minor, Melodic minor and Hungarian minor

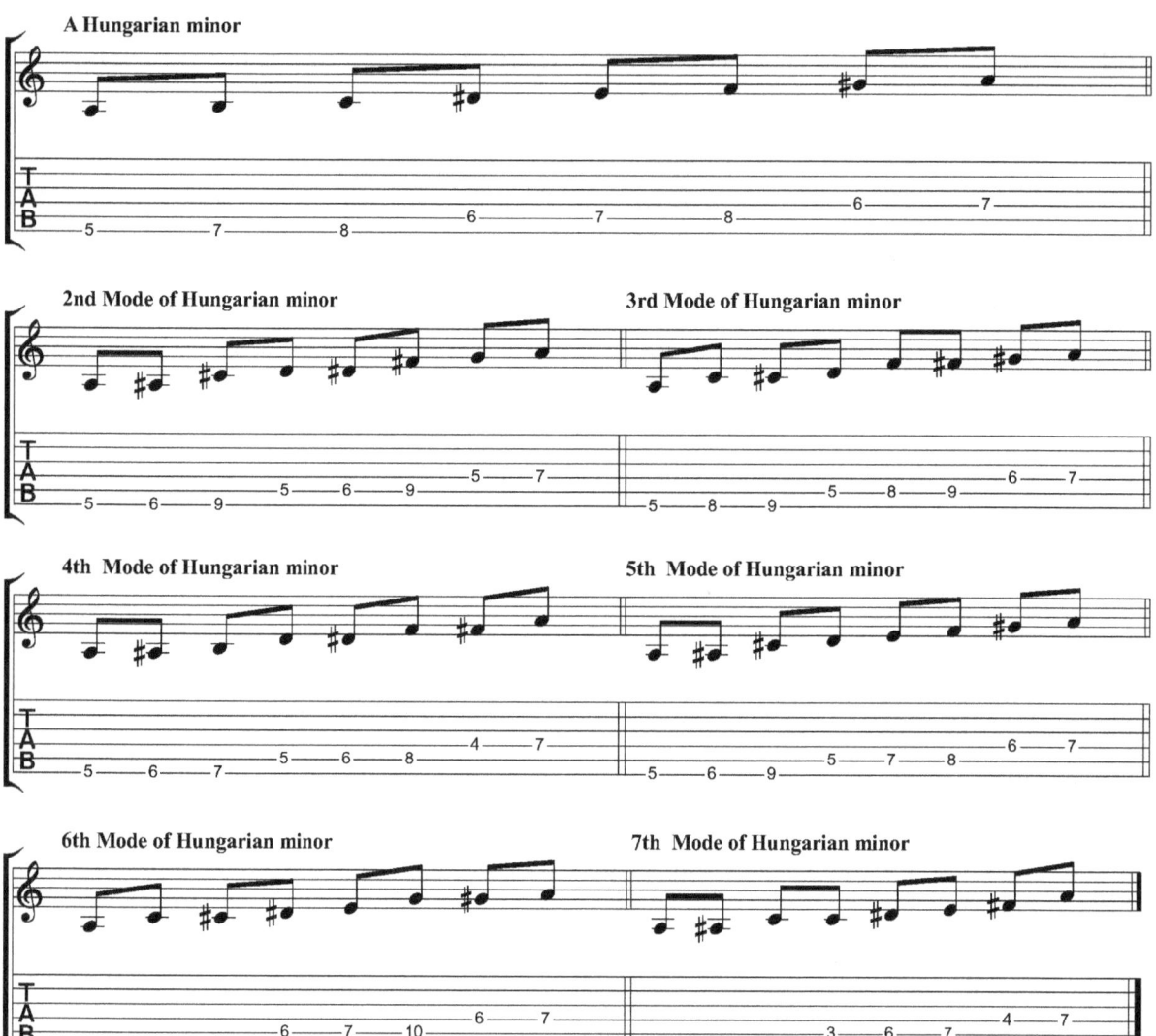

Diagonal Shapes Using Octaves

It is very easy to take an idea within one octave and make it a three octave idea because the shapes of the various fingerings on the guitar are the same an octave higher.

Mode Fingerings

7 Modes in A Minor
3 note per string fingerings

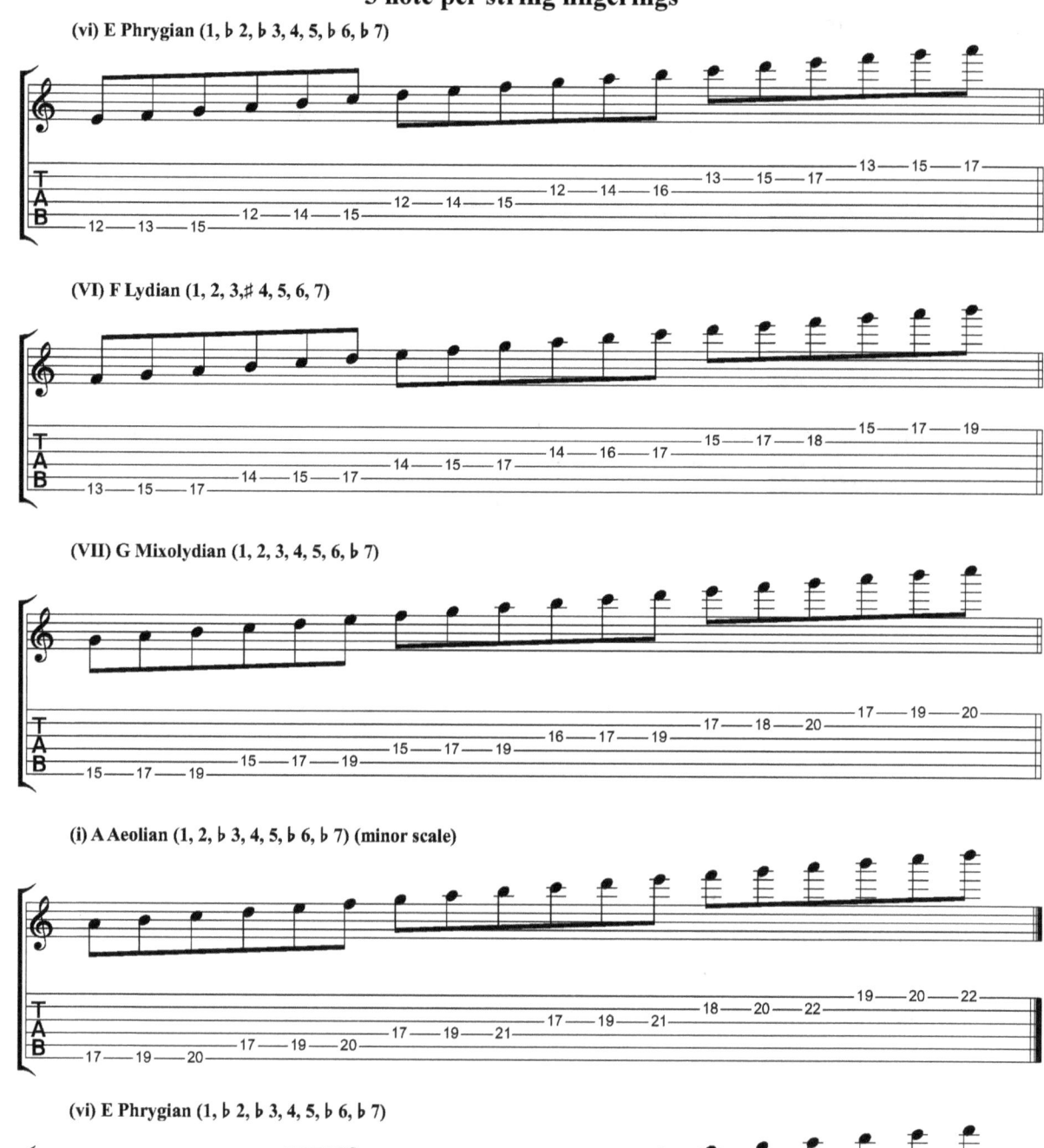

(VI) F Lydian (1, 2, 3, ♯ 4, 5, 6, 7)

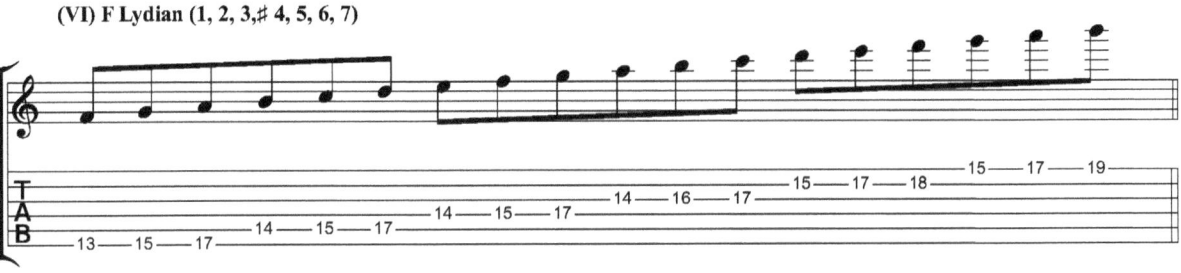

(VII) G Mixolydian (1, 2, 3, 4, 5, 6, ♭ 7)

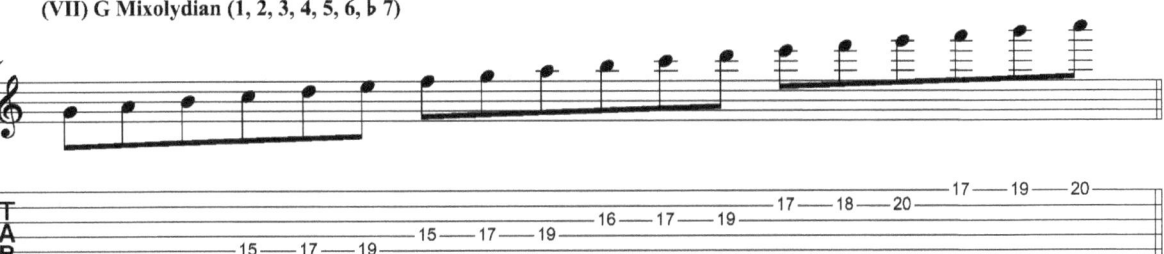

(i) A Aeolian (1, 2, ♭ 3, 4, 5, ♭ 6, ♭ 7) (minor scale)

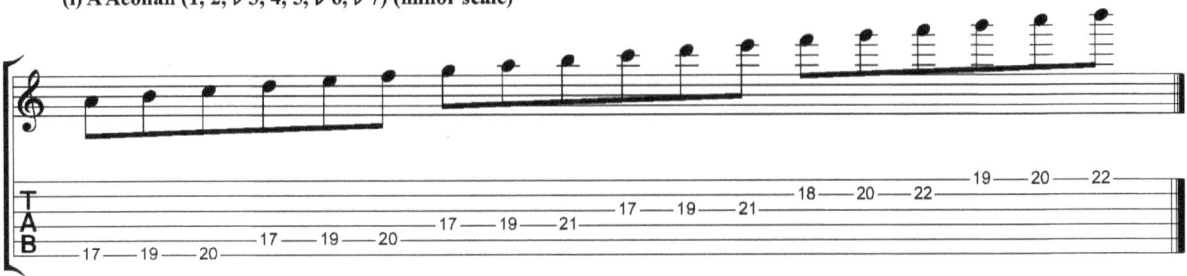

7 Modes in A Harmonic Minor
3 note per string fingerings

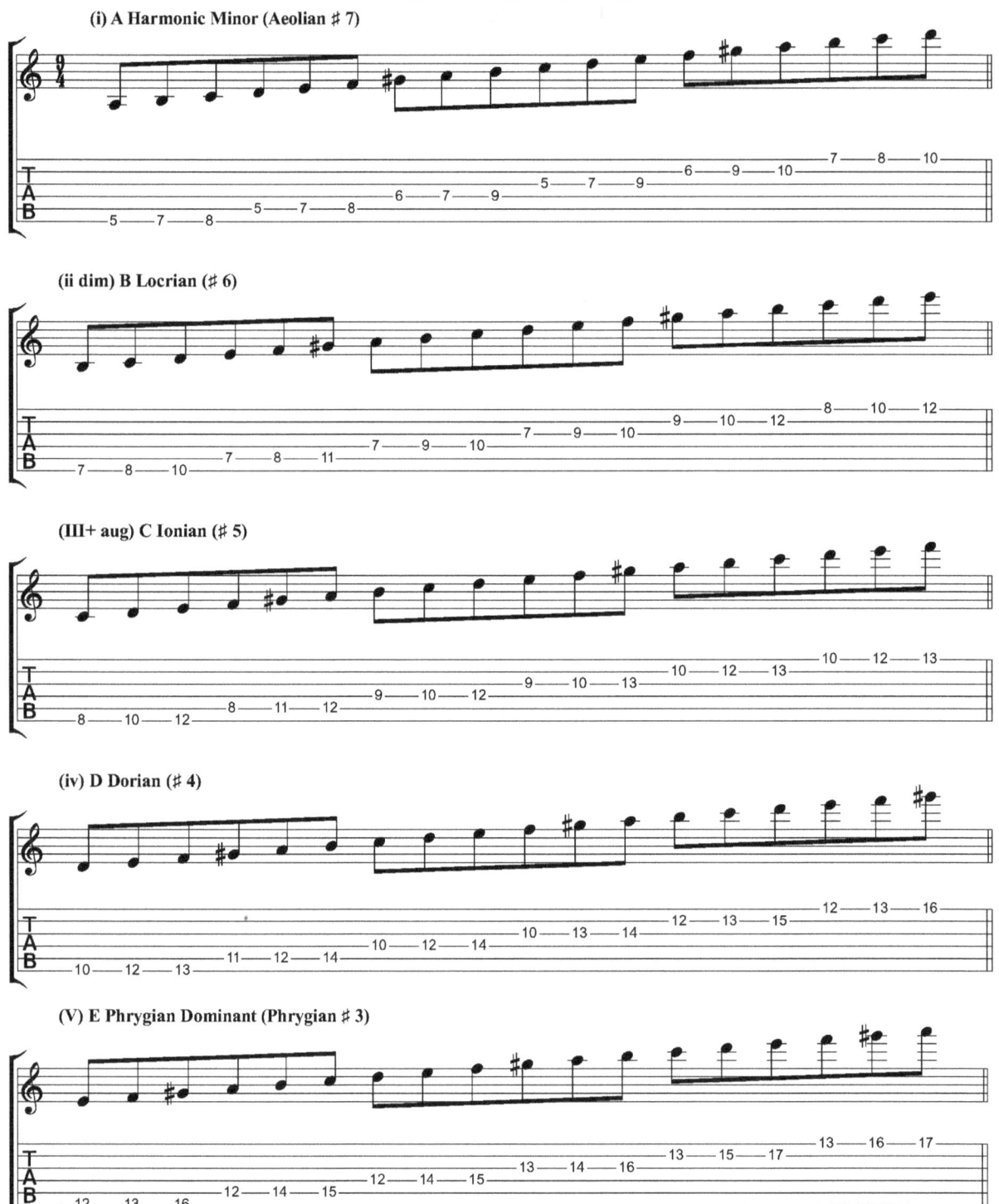

(VI) F Lydian (♯ 2)

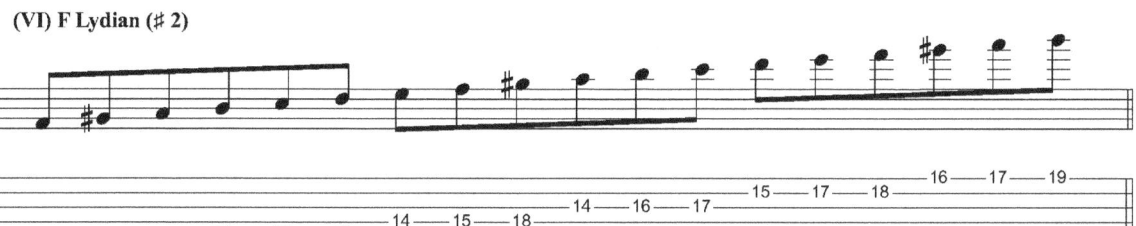

(vii dim) G♯ Mixolydian (♯ 1)

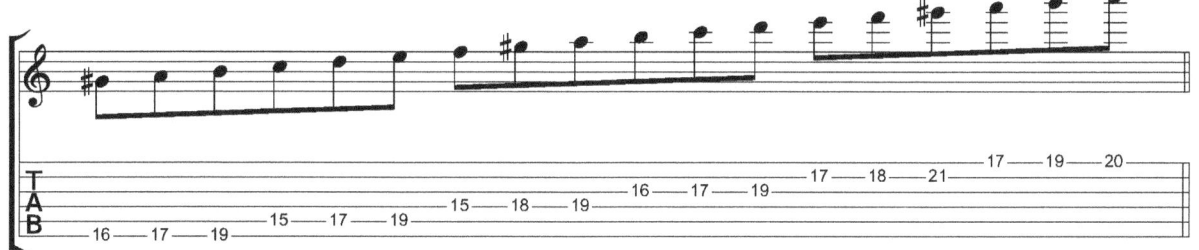

(i) A Harmonic Minor (Aeolian ♯ 7)

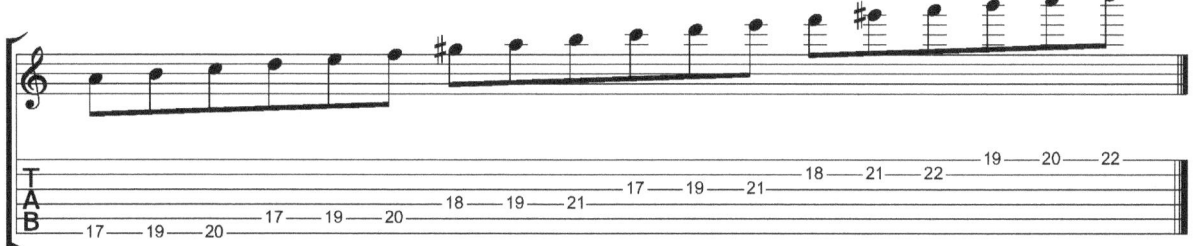

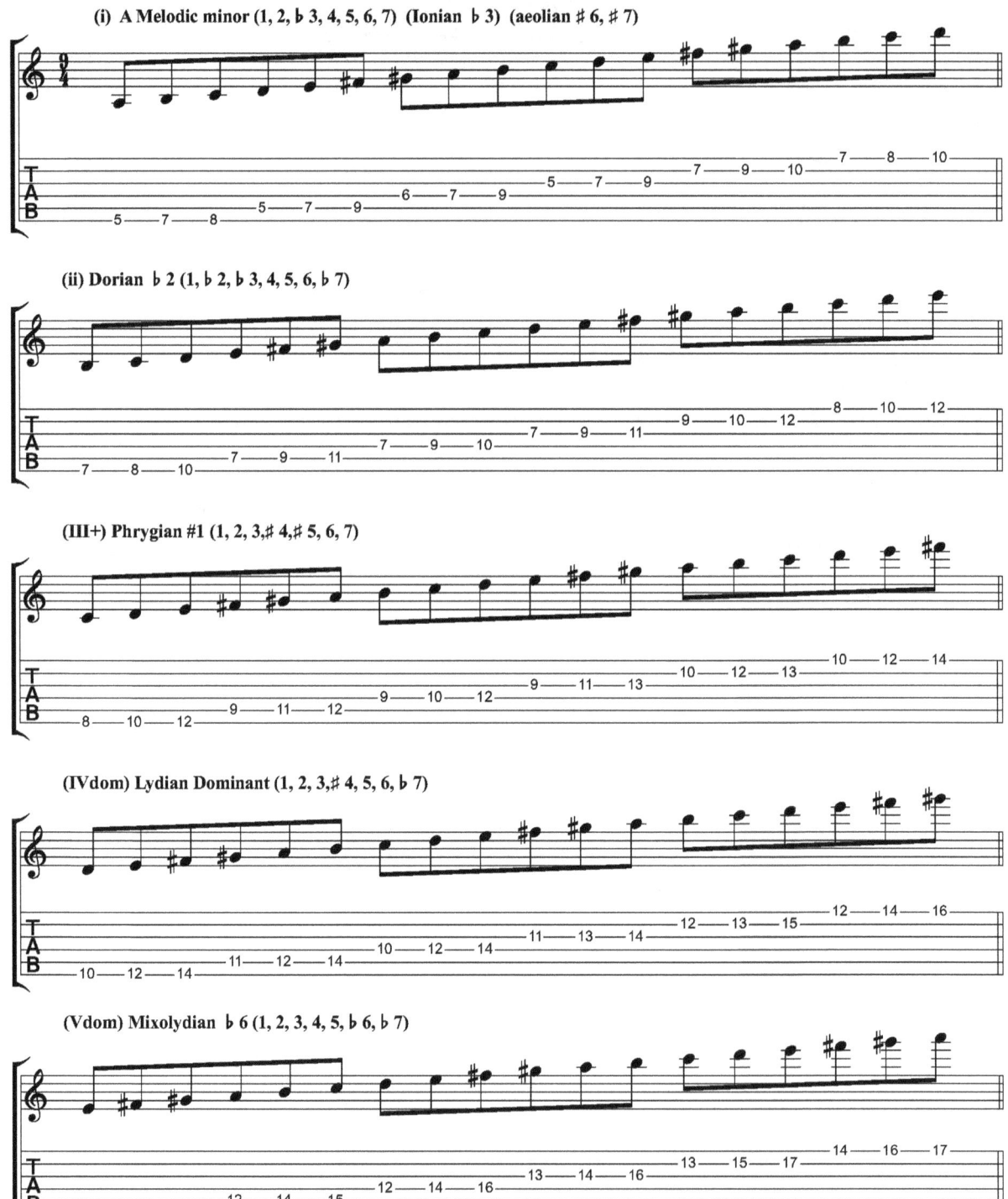

(vi dim) Aeolian ♭5 (1, 2, ♭3, 4, ♭5, ♭6, ♭7)

(vii dim/alt.dom) Super Locrian (1, ♭2, ♭3, ♯4, ♯5, ♭6 ♭7)

(i) A Melodic minor (1, 2, ♭3, 4, 5, 6, 7) (Ionian ♭3) (aeolian ♯6, ♯7)

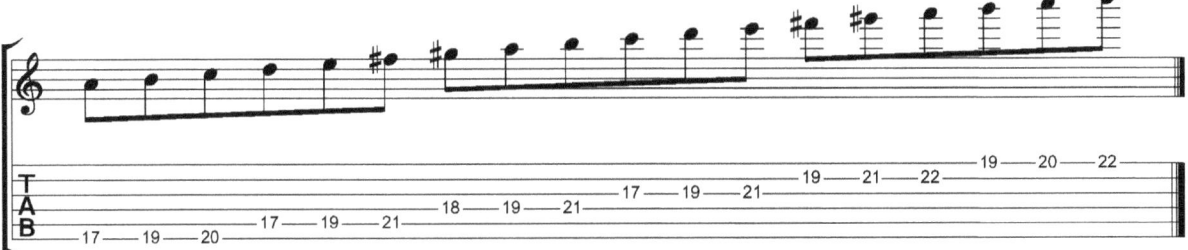

7 Modes in A Hungarian Minor
3 note per string fingerings

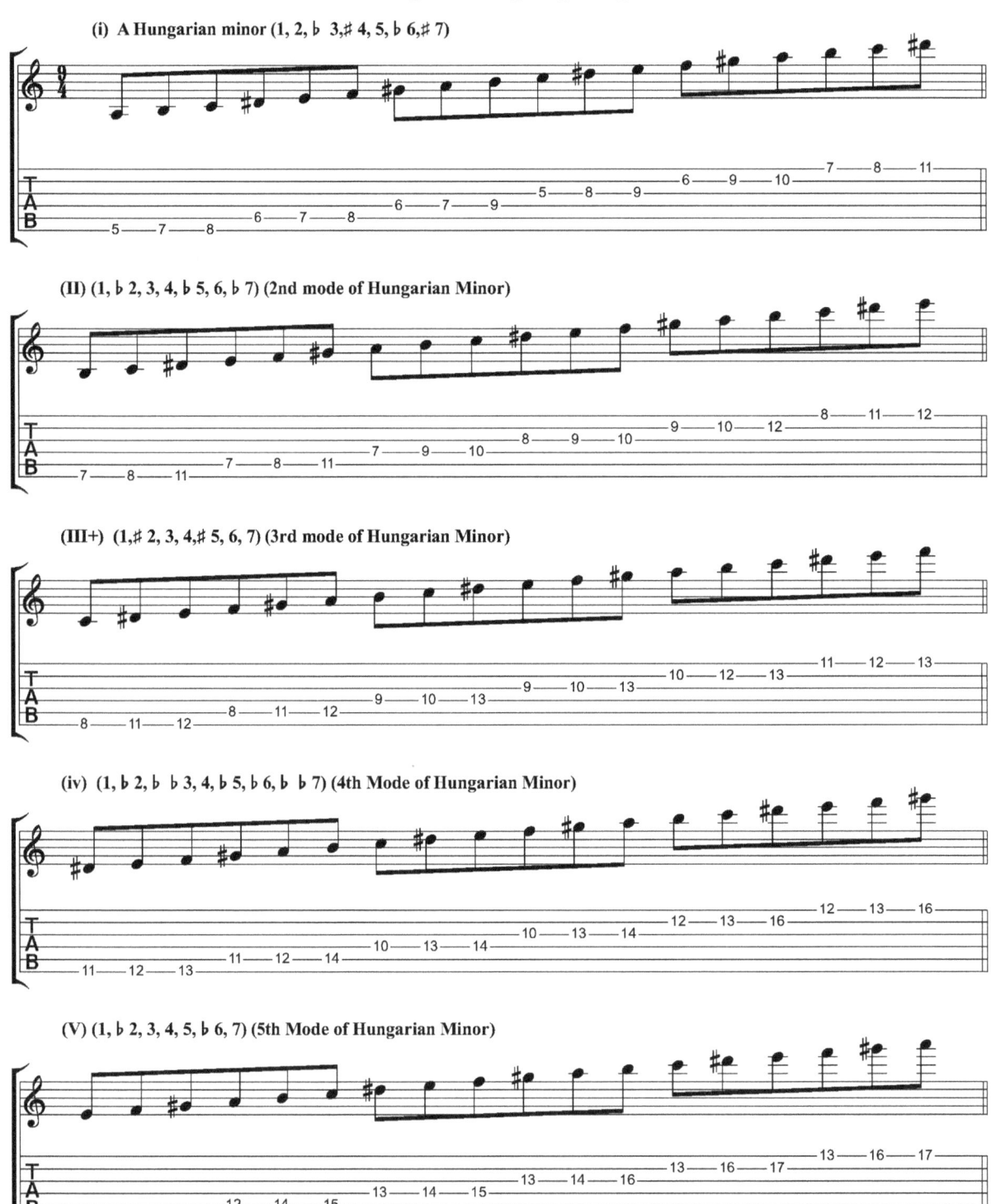

- 38 - *Mode Fingerings*

(vii) (1, ♭2, ♭3, ♭4, 5, ♭6, ♭♭7) 7th Mode of (Hungarian Minor)

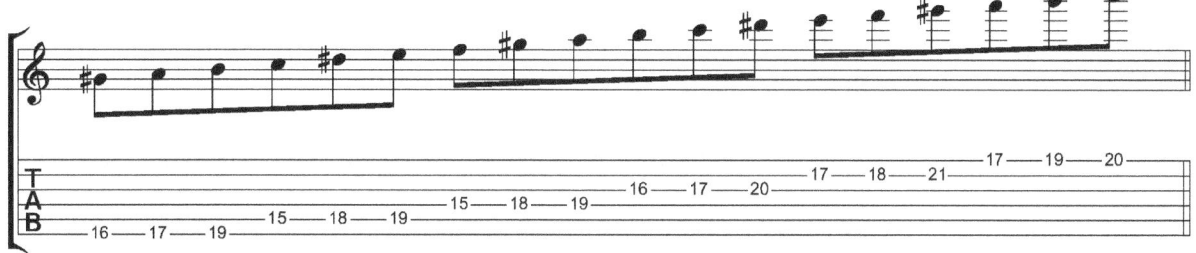

(i) A Hungarian minor (1, 2, ♭3, #4, 5, ♭6, #7)

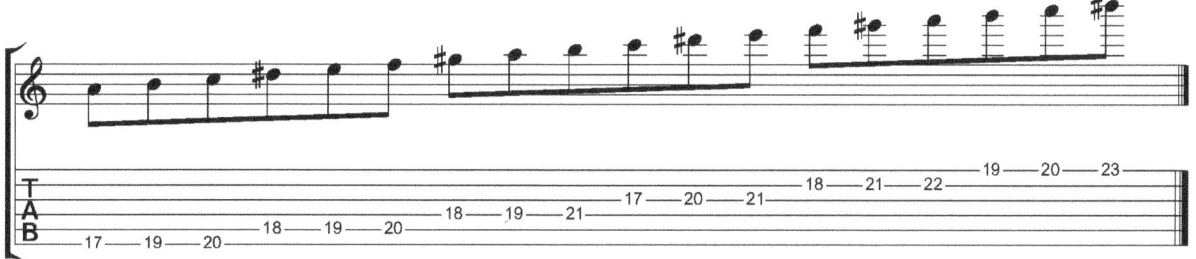

Conventional Mode Fingerings

Good for jazz, blues and country, the conventional fingerings keep you around one position of the neck. They work well for reading and for mixing them within your pentatonic boxes.

Another good exercise to understand the different feelings that each mode evokes is to play over one note in the background (a drone), perhaps even an A note from a tuner. I used to use the dial tone from my telephone. Then play all the different modes from the same root, in this case A. So, play some notes out of A Ionian, then A Dorian, then A Phrygian, etc. Listen for the difference in vibe. Learning the vibes and feelings is far more important than learning the fingerings throughout the neck.

It is also very important to have a personal relationship with each mode. If you understand the feeling that each mode evokes in the listener then you are well on your way to learning the true magick of modes. It is better to remember the modes by feelings, intervals, and by knowing what mode (or modes) various songs and melodies are in. This is much more precise than using words to describe them. However, here I will try to describe them in words for you. Ionian has a happy, plain, childlike vibe. Dorian has a darker vibe and is somewhat milky sounding. Phrygian sounds eastern and, perhaps, even scary. Lydian is somewhat mystical and somewhat strange. Mixolydian has a happy, psychedelic vibe to it. Aeolian is very sad. Locrian is a very dark, frantic mode, and is somewhat hard to place.

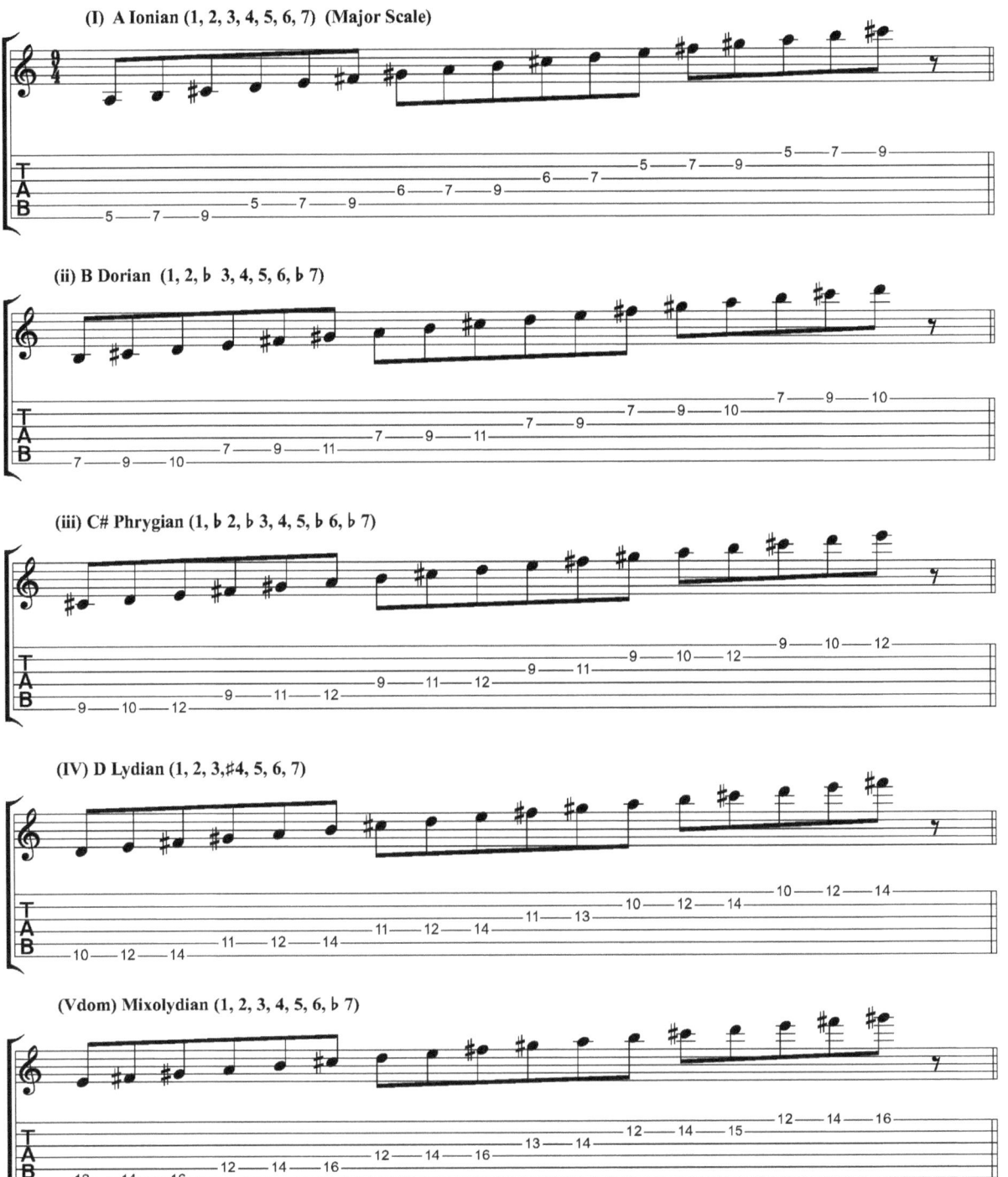

- 42 - **Conventional Mode Fingerings**

Arpeggio Fingerings

Arpeggios can be played many ways on the guitar. Here is a very easy way to figure out where all the notes are throughout the neck for any major, minor, diminished, or augmented arpeggio. Just like the chords, there are only three different notes in any major, minor, diminished, or augmented arpeggio, this allows us to be able to learn only three different fingerings for any of these arpeggios. These are essentially just inversions of arpeggios. This method will get us the entire fingerboard for any arpeggio. We must memorize where the root notes are for each shape, and we must memorize which shape comes before and after each shape. It is also very important to break these shapes into two string runs, patterns and licks by playing only the notes on the high E and B strings up and down the neck in the three different fingerings. Then try only the top three strings for three string arpeggios, then the top four, then the top five, and then finally learn to play long six string arpeggios. This progression is very helpful in learning sweep picking as well. The fingerboard maps of chords/arpeggios and seventh chords/arpeggios at the end of this section can be used to create your own chord voicings as well as your own arpeggio fingerings. This map may also allow you to see some patterns and shapes to help connect the entire fingerboard for chords and arpeggios.

Arpeggios as 3 string shapes

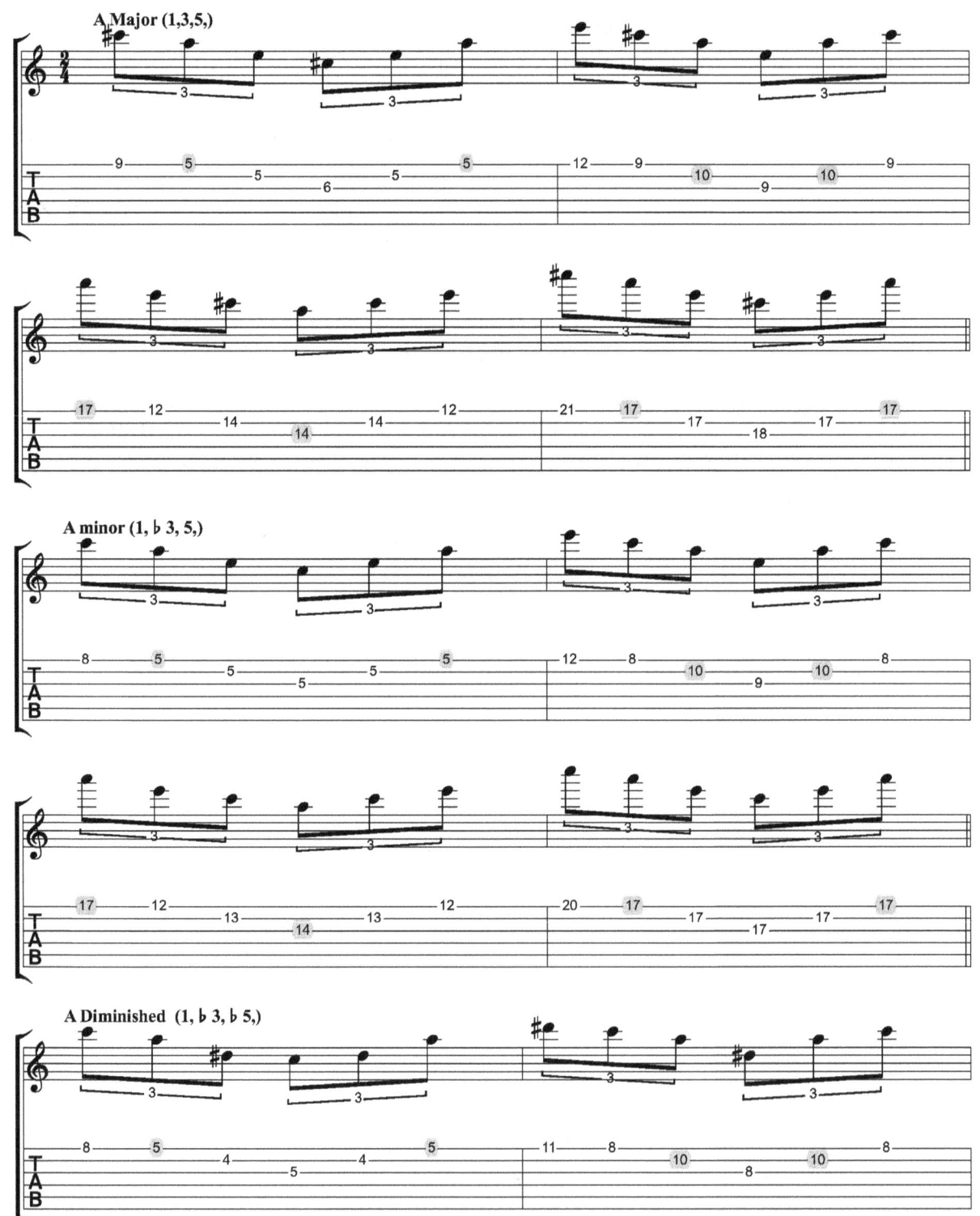

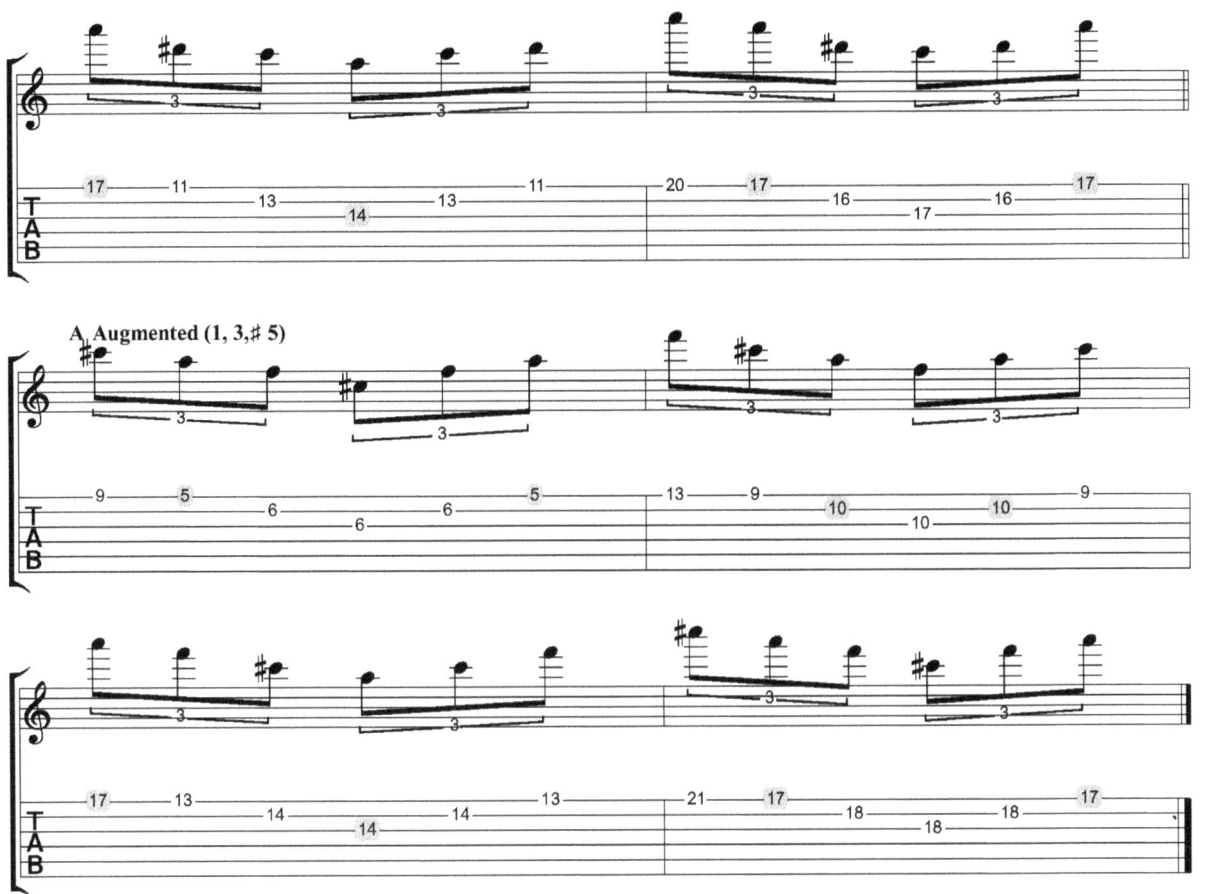

Arpeggios as 4 string shapes

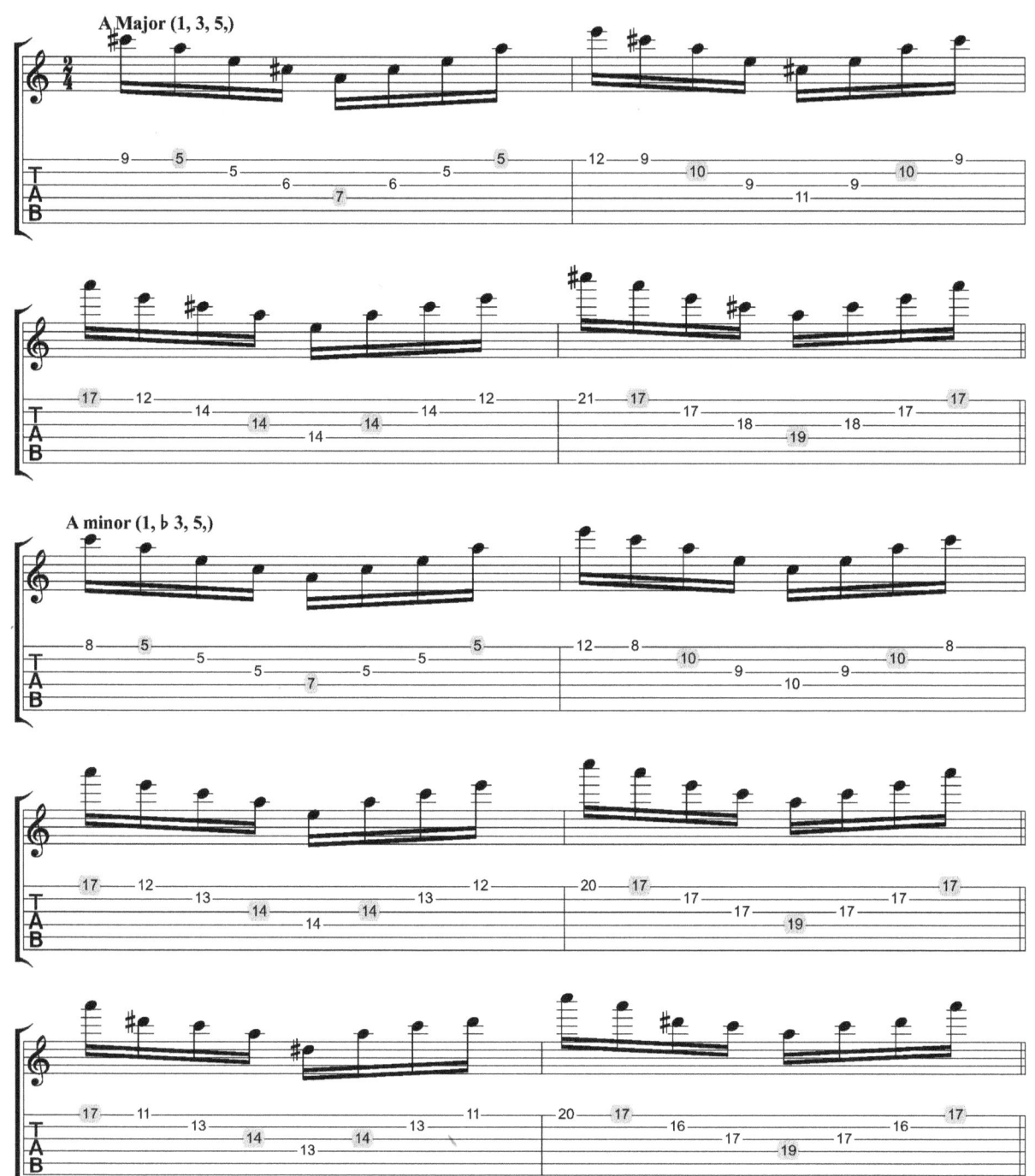

- 46 - *Arpeggio Fingerings*

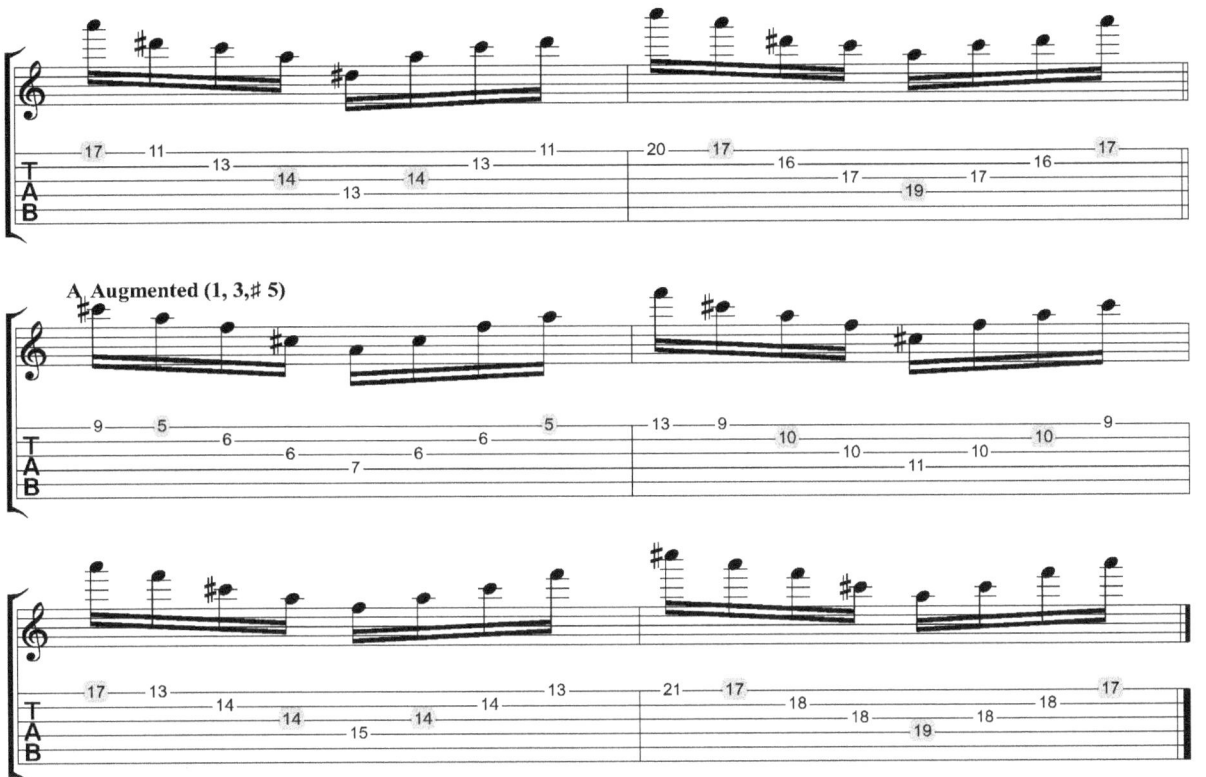

Guitar in Theory and Practice - 47 -

Arpeggios as 5 string shapes

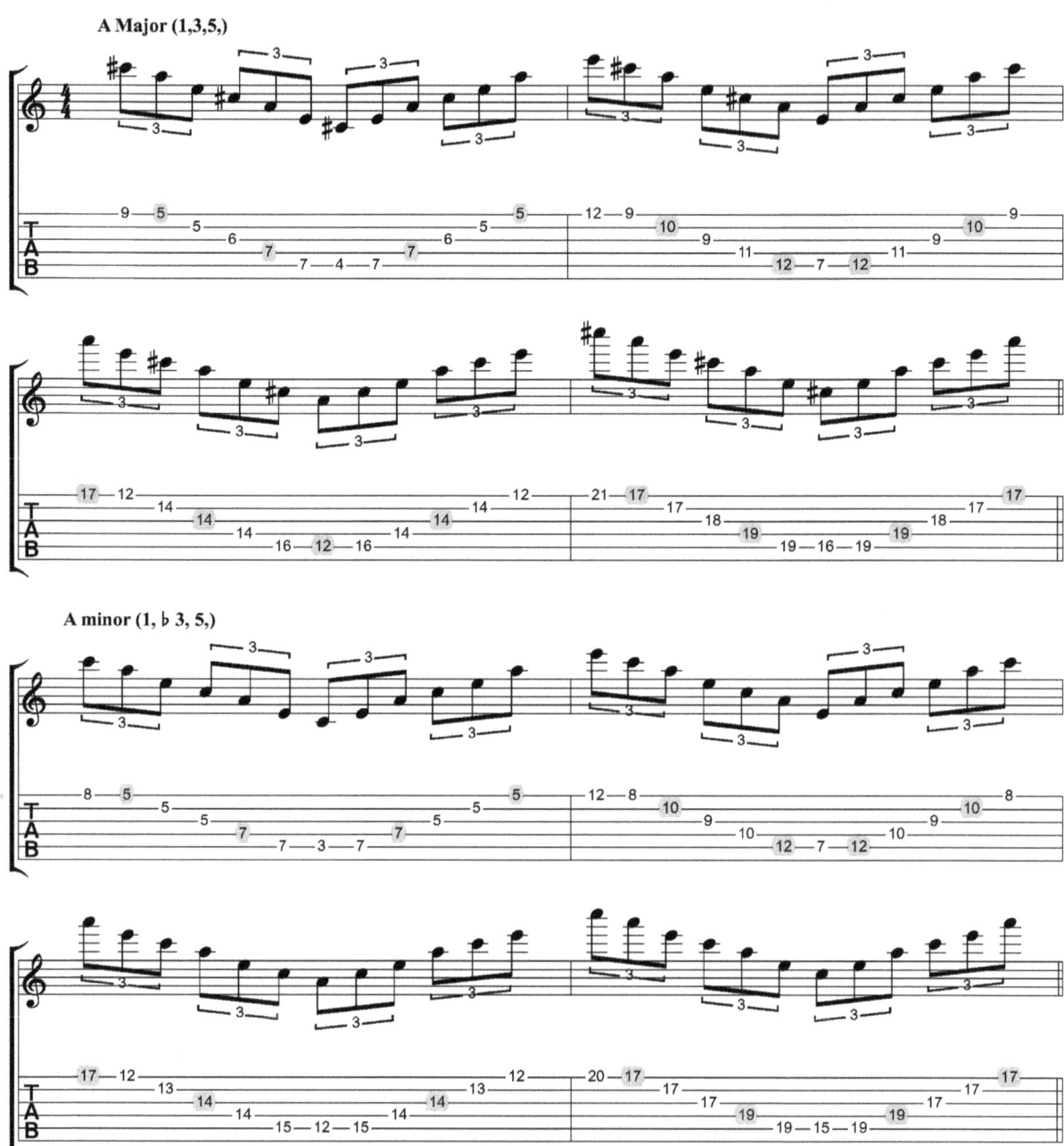

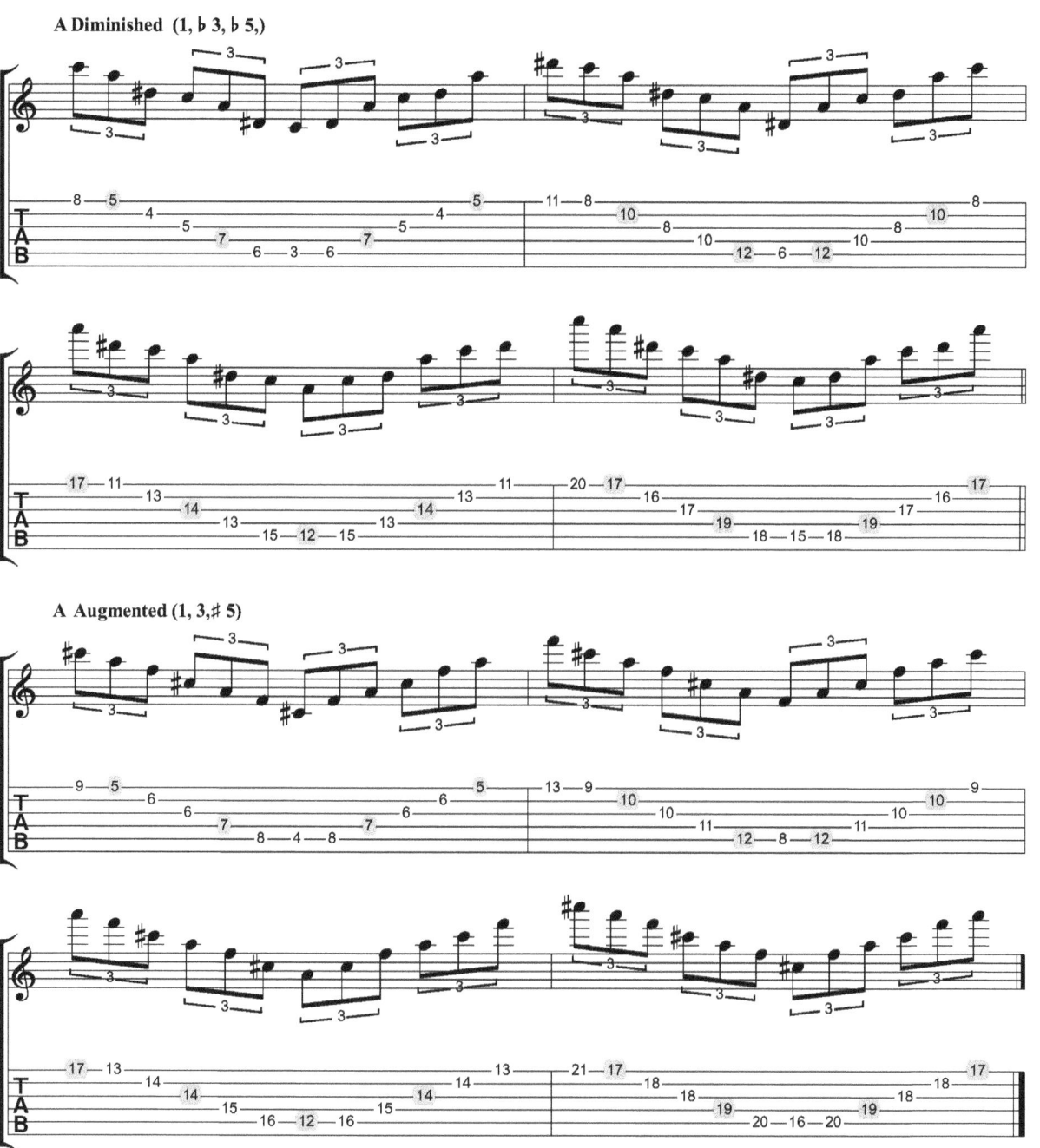

Arpeggios as 6 string shapes

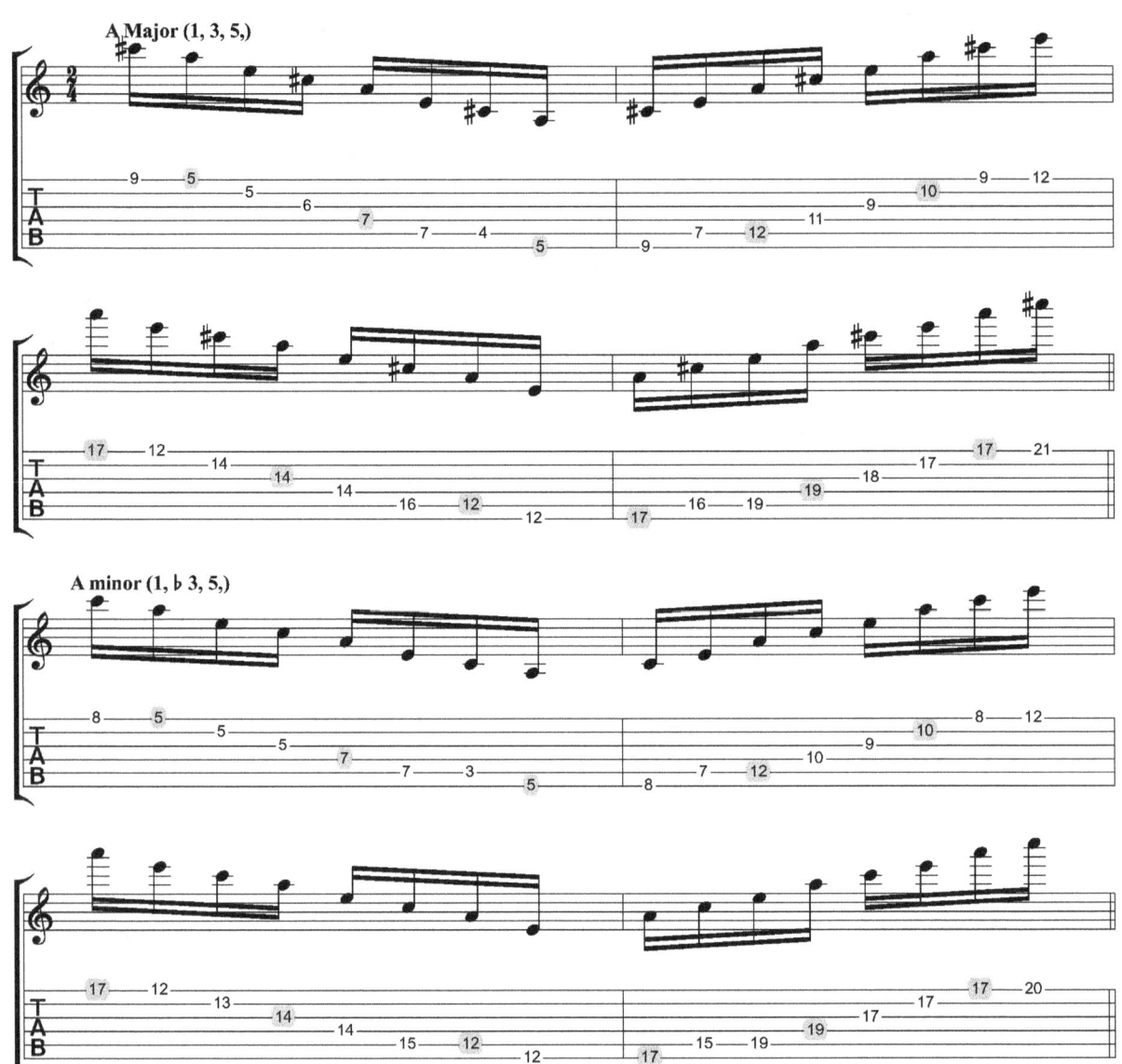

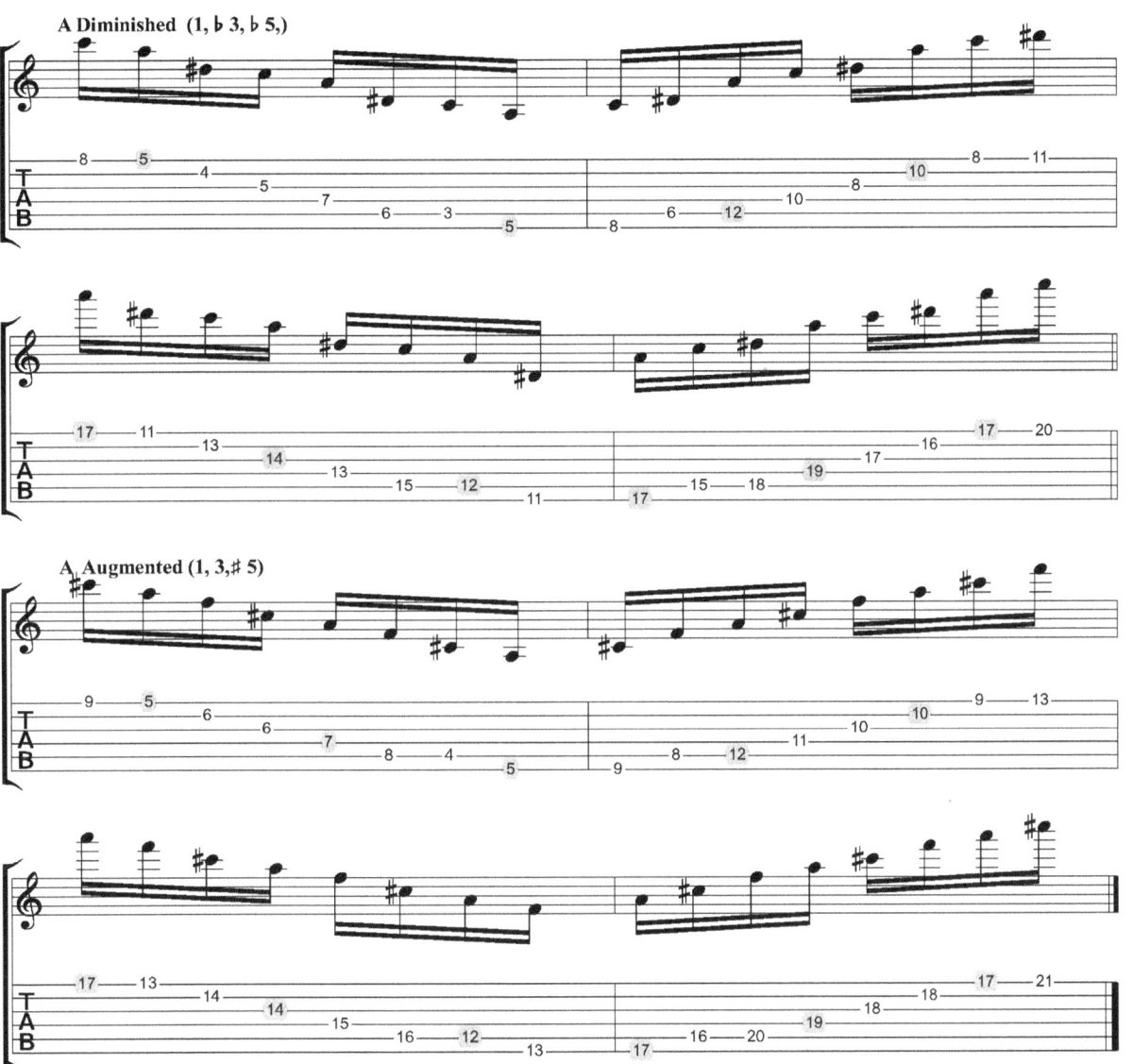

Seventh Arpeggio Fingerings

Learning seventh arpeggios is very similar to learning the basic arpeggios (triads). There are four different notes in any seventh arpeggio, so we must memorize four different shapes. Again, we must memorize where the root notes are for each shape, and we must memorize which shape comes before and after each shape. Playing fast seventh arpeggios has always been very difficult for guitar players to learn. I have devised these fingerings to allow for you to play them insanely fast with economy picking.

Once you can play any arpeggio in time, learn how to change from one arpeggio to any other arpeggio in generally the same position in time. That is why it is important to have some stock 8th note, triplet, 16th note, sextuplet and possibly 32nd note licks prepared. Try to learn to sequence them over common chord progressions in time, and then you will be ready to use them in your solos.

I think it is essential that you learn and study chords/arpeggios and scales. However, you must not just learn the fingerings and play the scales up and down. You must learn to improvise with them. You must learn to make them sound like music.

3 String Seventh Arpeggios

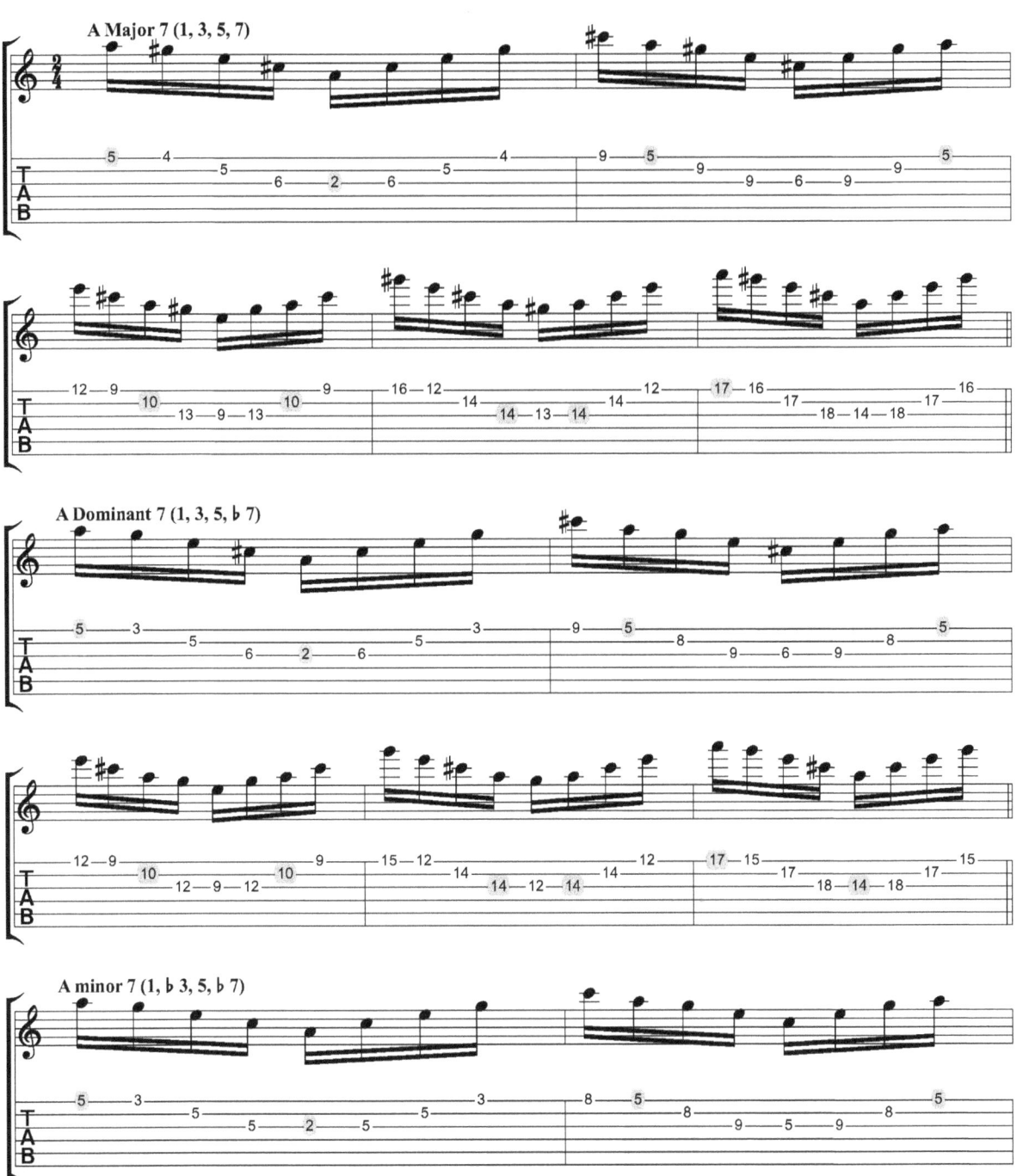

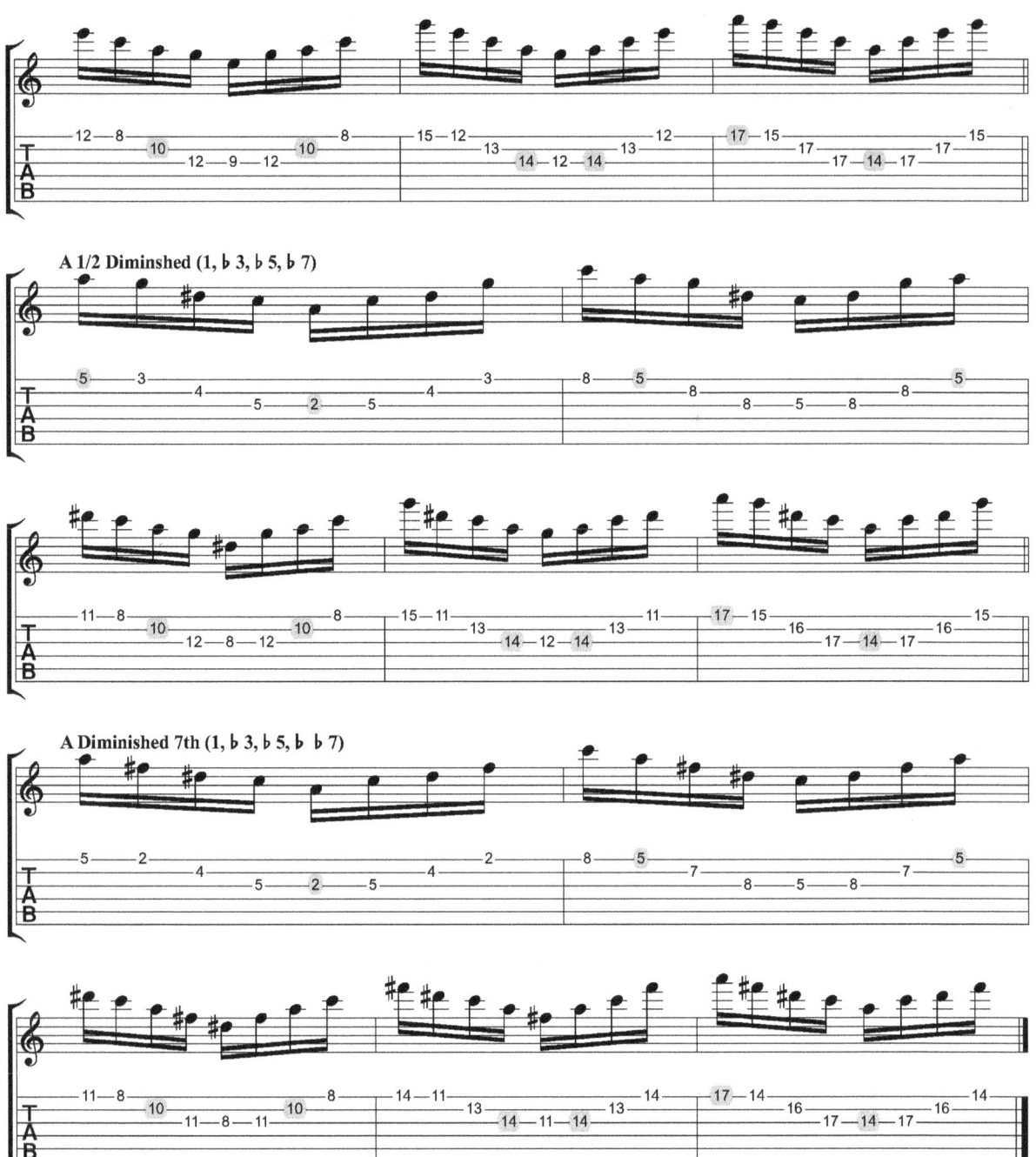

5 String Seventh Arpeggios

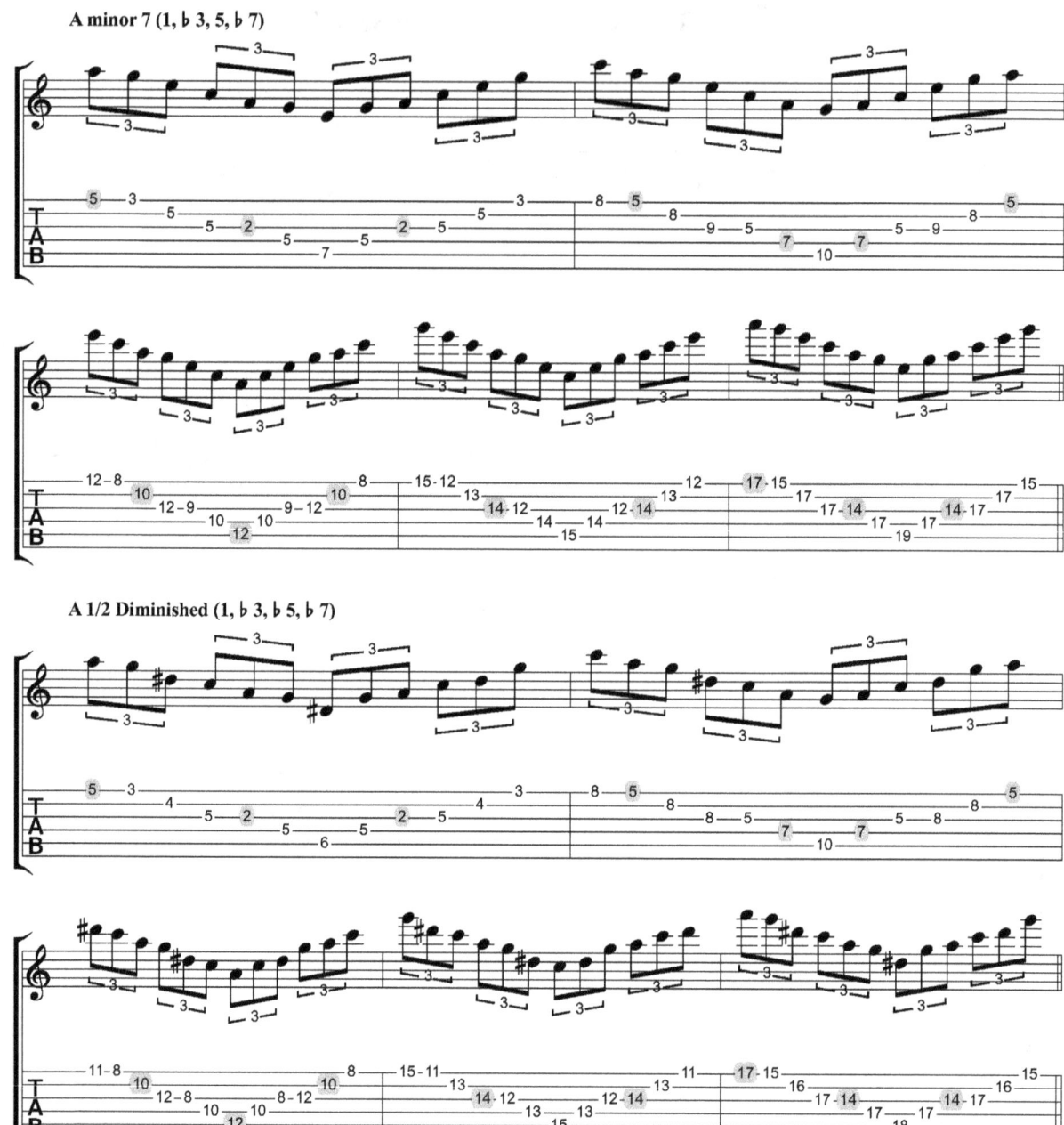

A Diminished 7th (1, ♭3, ♭5, ♭♭7)

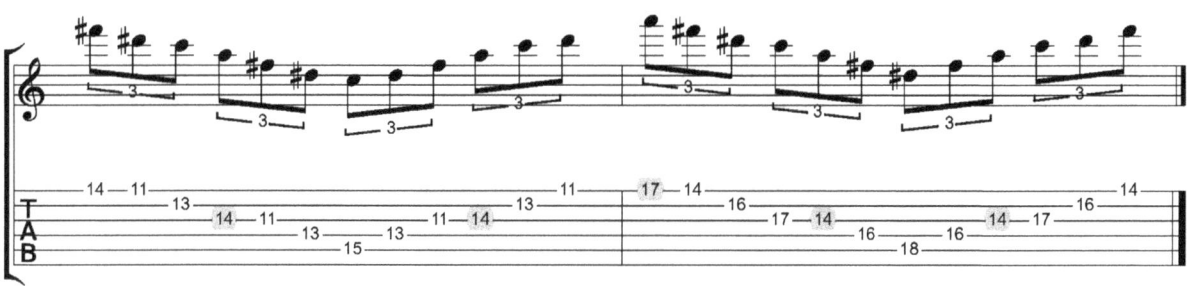

6 String Seventh Arpeggios

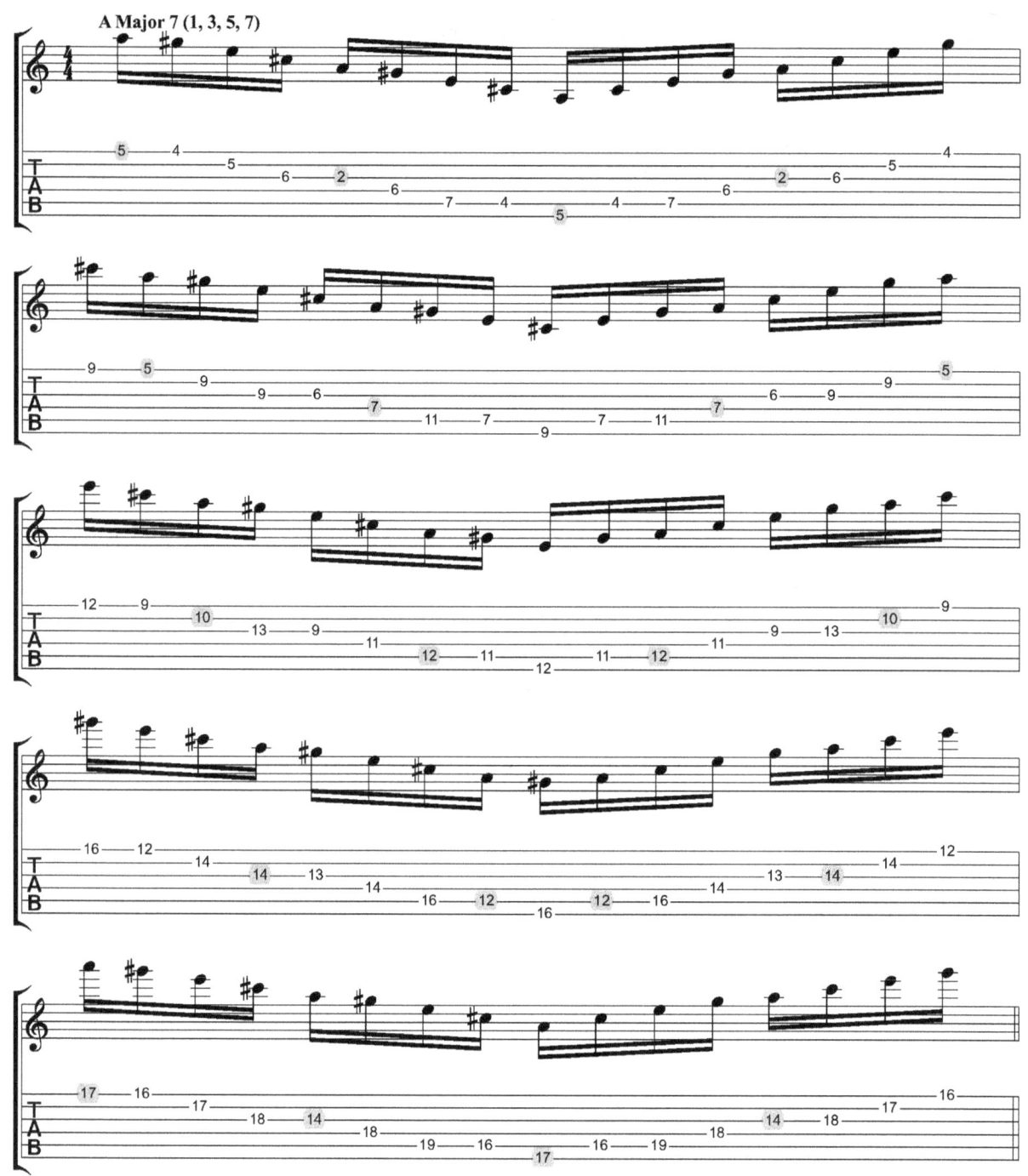

- 58 - Seventh Arpeggio Fingerings

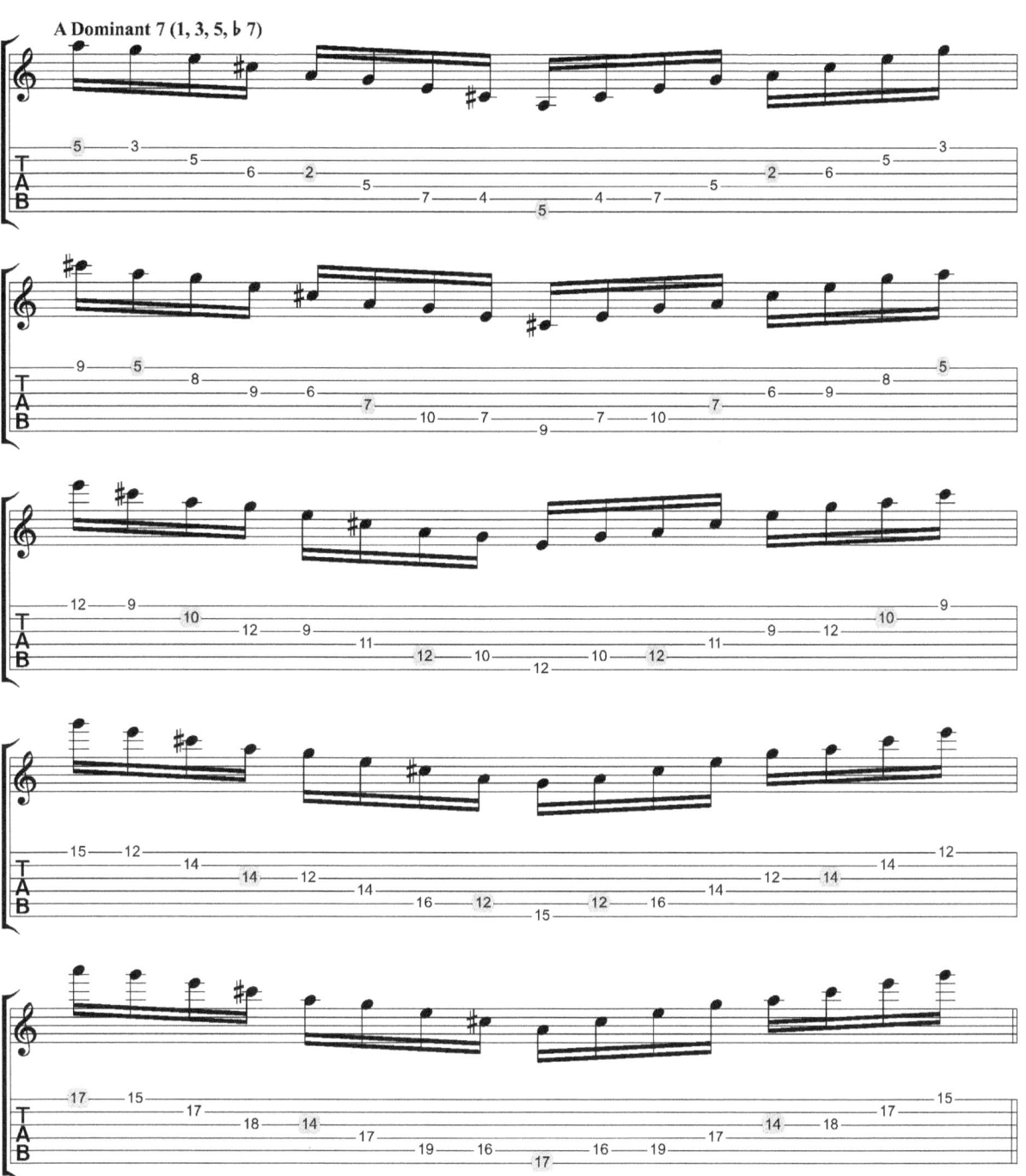

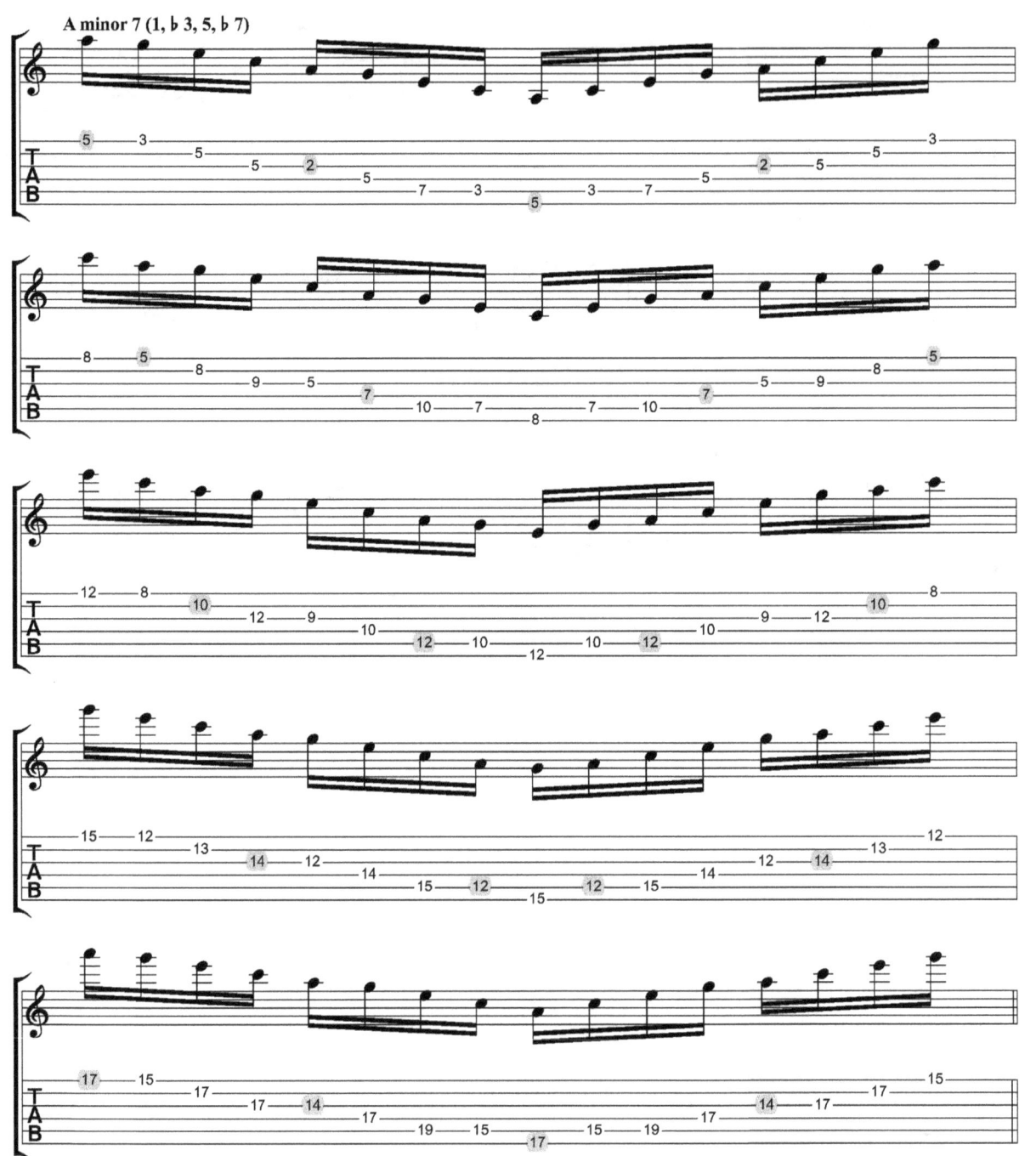

A 1/2 Diminished (1, ♭3, ♭5, ♭7)

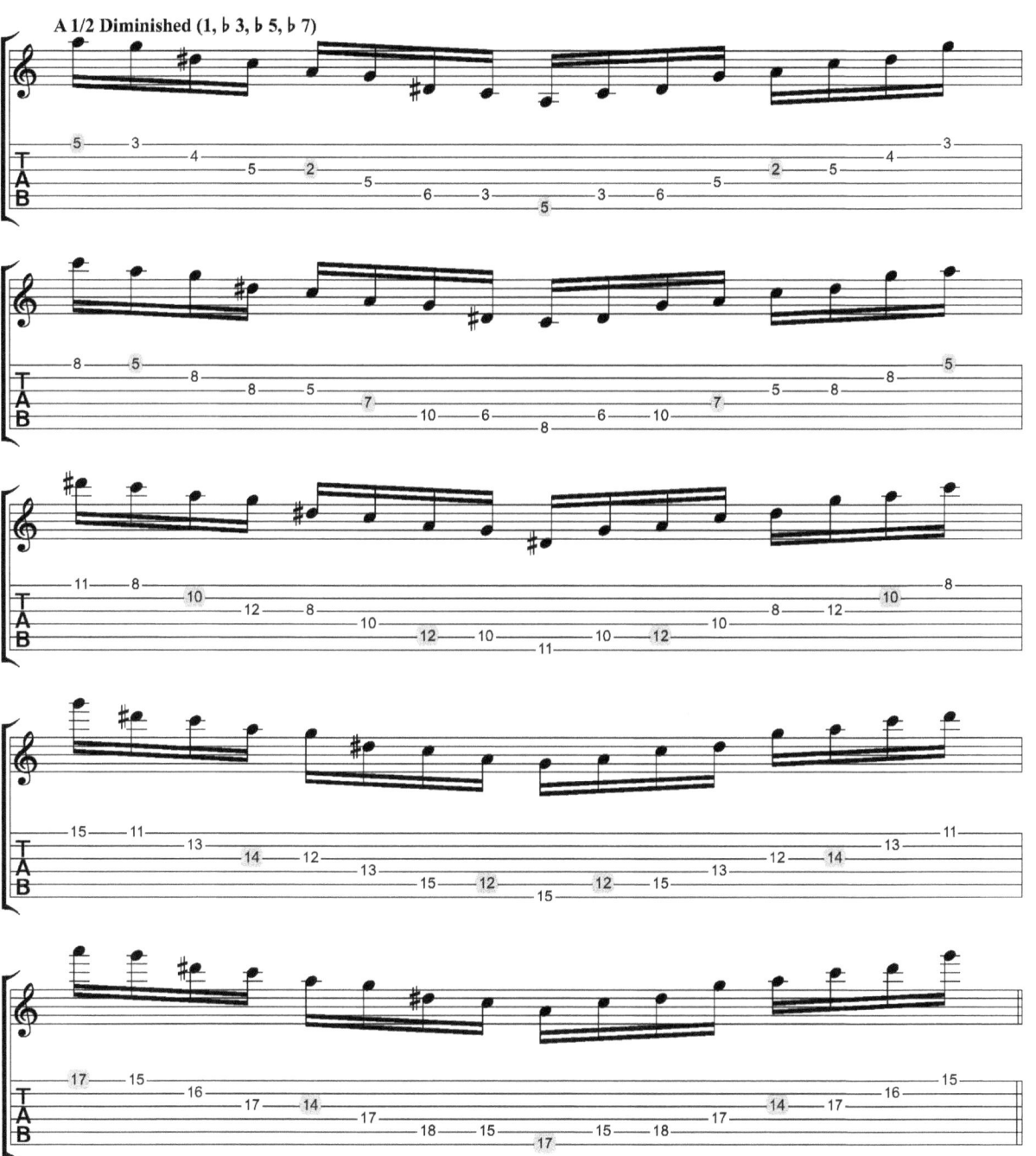

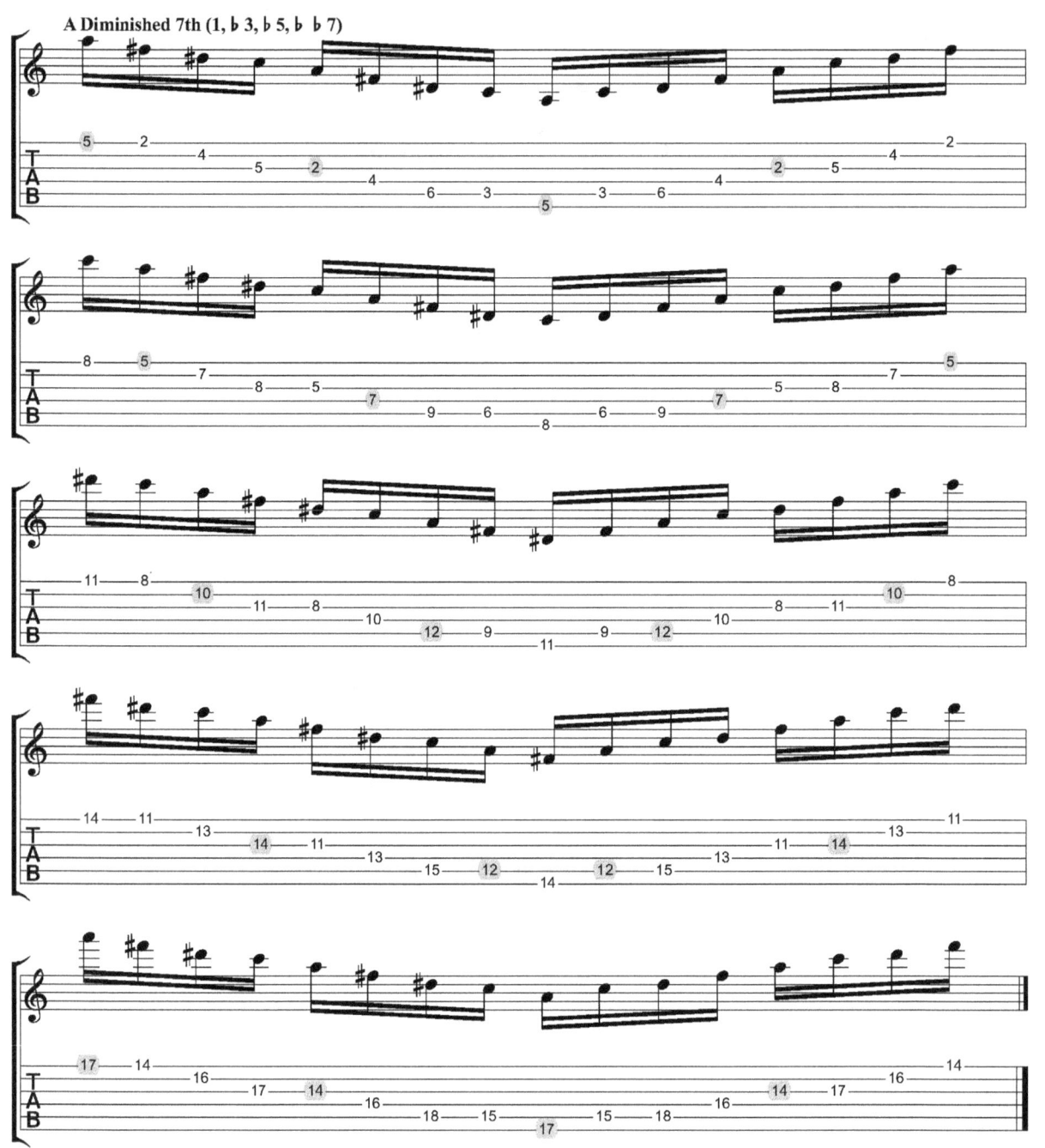

Chords, Arpeggios, and Seventh Chords

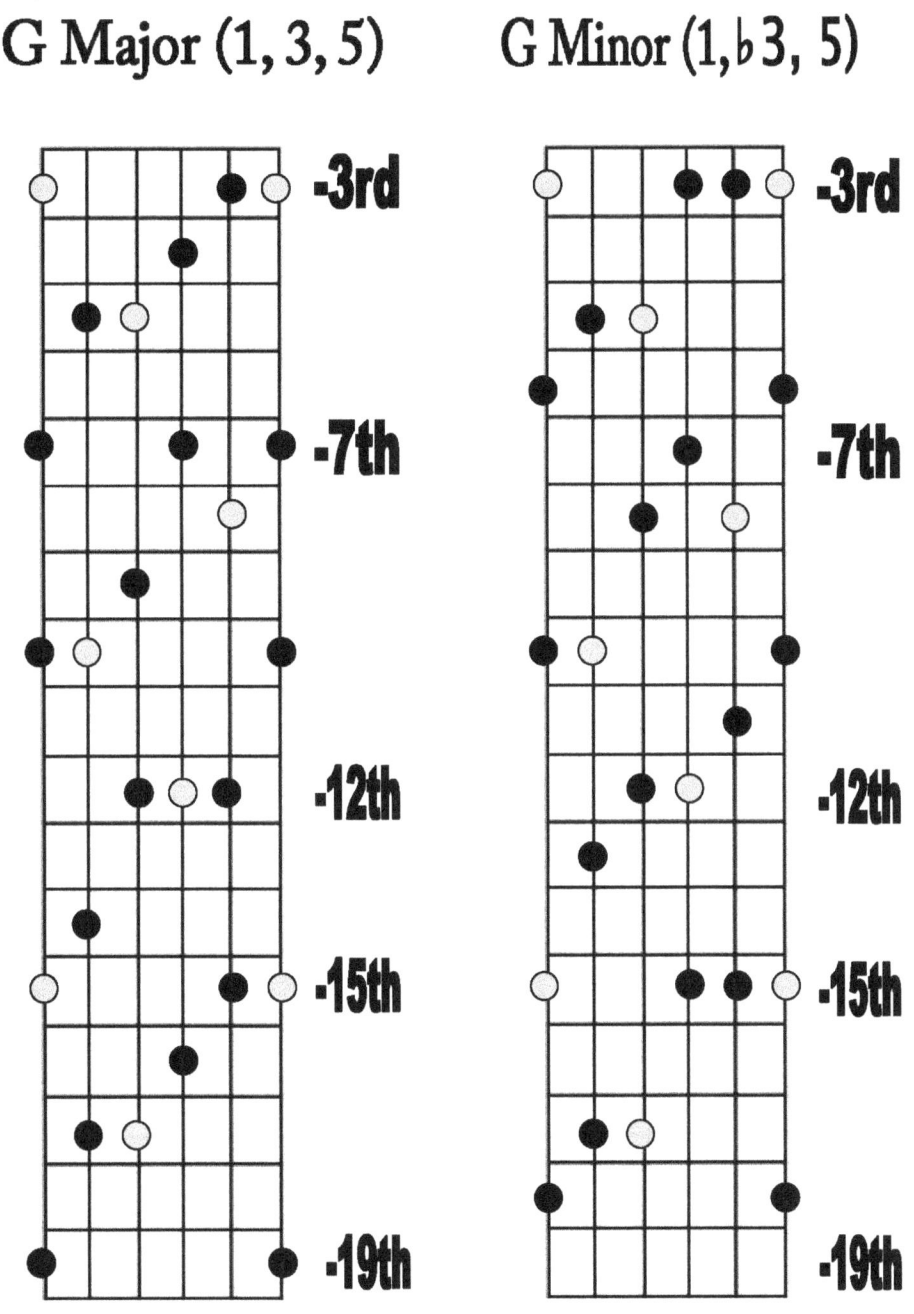

G diminished (1, ♭3, ♭5)   G Augmented (1, 3, ♯5)

-3rd

-7th

-12th

-15th

-19th

- 64 - Chords, Arpeggios, and Seventh Chords

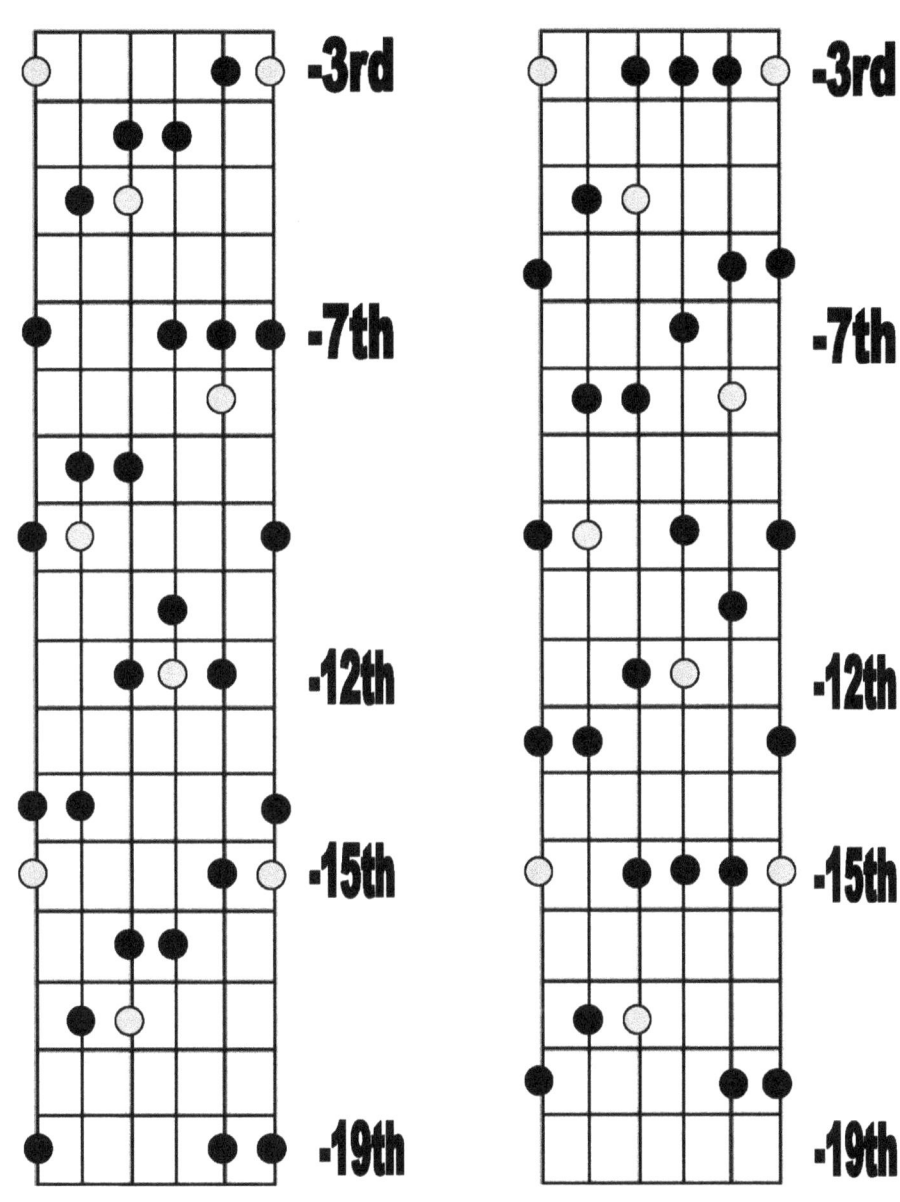

G dominant 7 (1, 3, 5, ♭7)

G 1/2 diminished (1, ♭3, ♭5, ♭7)

G Diminished 7th (1,♭3,♭5,♭♭7)

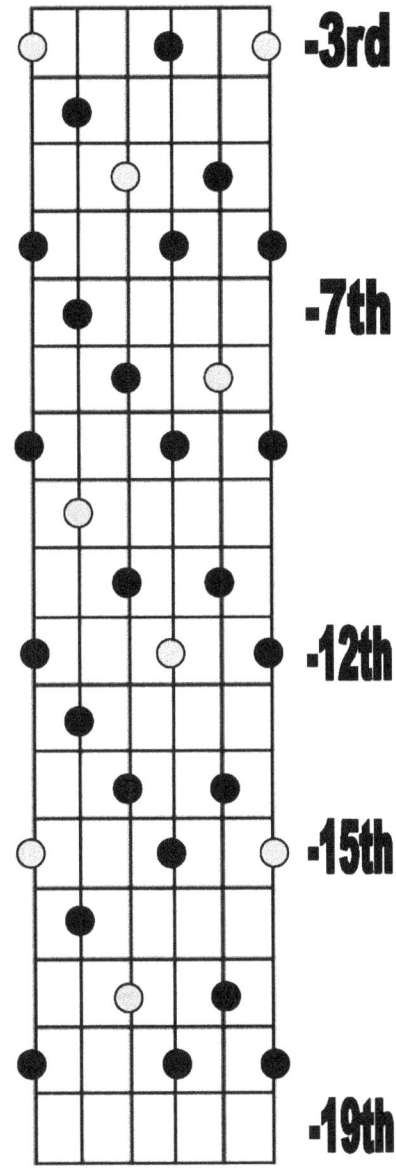

Diff'rent Strokes (Alternate Picking Licks)

Whatchu talkin' 'bout? I'll tell you what I'm talkin' 'bout Arnold. I'm talkin' 'bout some good ole fashioned flatpickin' here, son! Playing fast is what will impress most people and some animals. So, here, let me help you with that.

Try to pick any note over and over as fast as you can. This is called tremolo picking. To do this, try picking with a downstroke, then an upstroke, then a downstroke, then an upstroke, etc. Alternate picking, of course, uses *diff'rent strokes* for every other note played. To play really fast using alternate picking you must get your two hands in sync together. Then you must be able to handle shifting strings and changing positions. Try these licks first as triplets, then as sextuplets to learn how to shred alternate picking style. Try them with hammer-ons and pull-offs to work on legato technique, and to build left hand strength.

Alternate Picking Licks

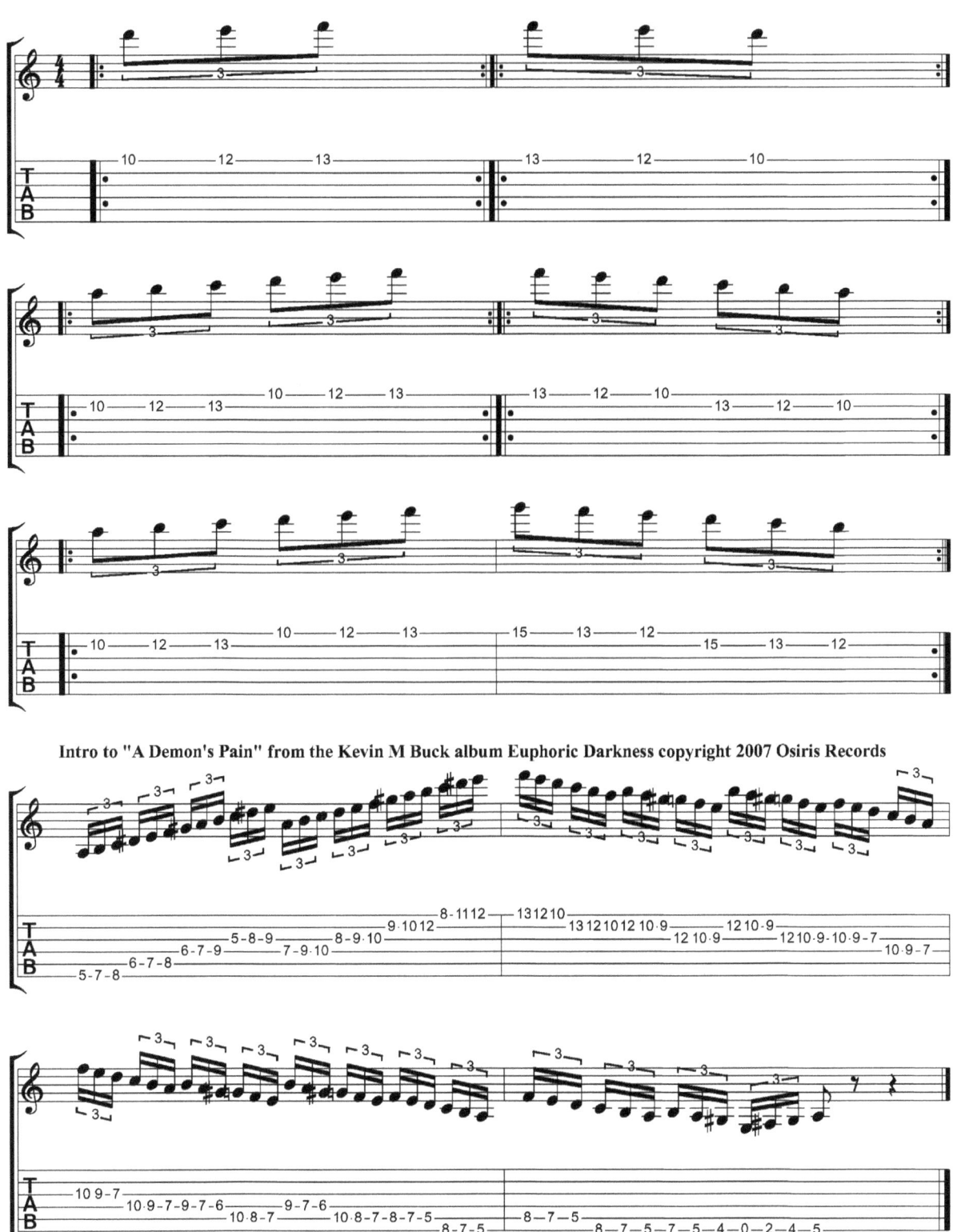

Intro to "A Demon's Pain" from the Kevin M Buck album Euphoric Darkness copyright 2007 Osiris Records

Licks, Sequences, and Runs

I have found that in any style of music there are three common melodic patterns that I always tend to hear. Try these patterns with slurs and various types of picking techniques. Try playing these patterns on only one string. Try them in all other scales and arpeggios that you know, as well. Listen for them in melodies and in solos that you hear. I recommend trying to see the pattern within the scale fingering rather than memorizing the whole pattern solely from the notation or tablature.

Licks, Sequences, and Runs
3 note, 4 note, and up 2 down 1

3 Note pattern in A minor

Licks, Sequences, and Runs

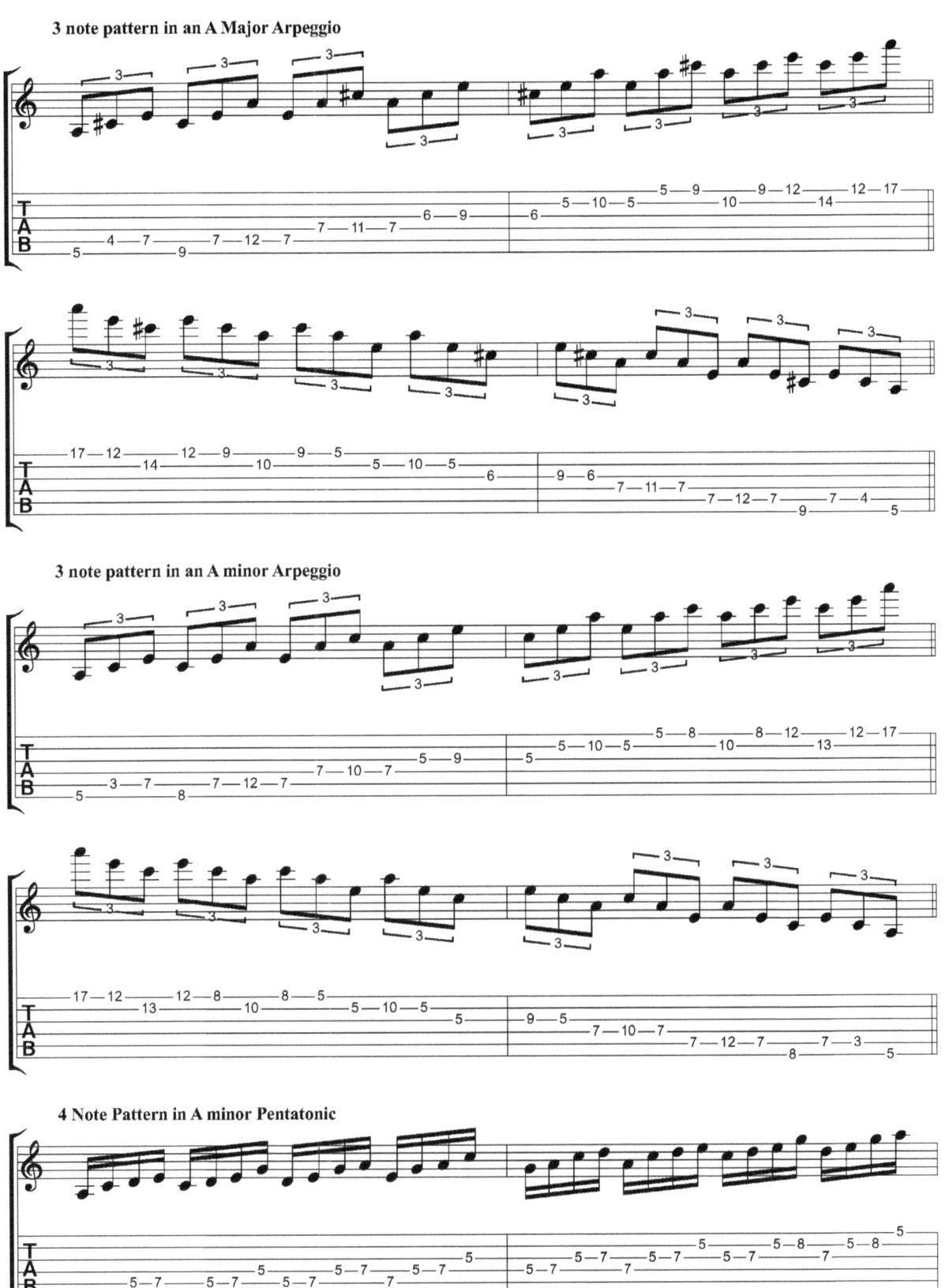

4 Note pattern in A Major

Licks, Sequences, and Runs

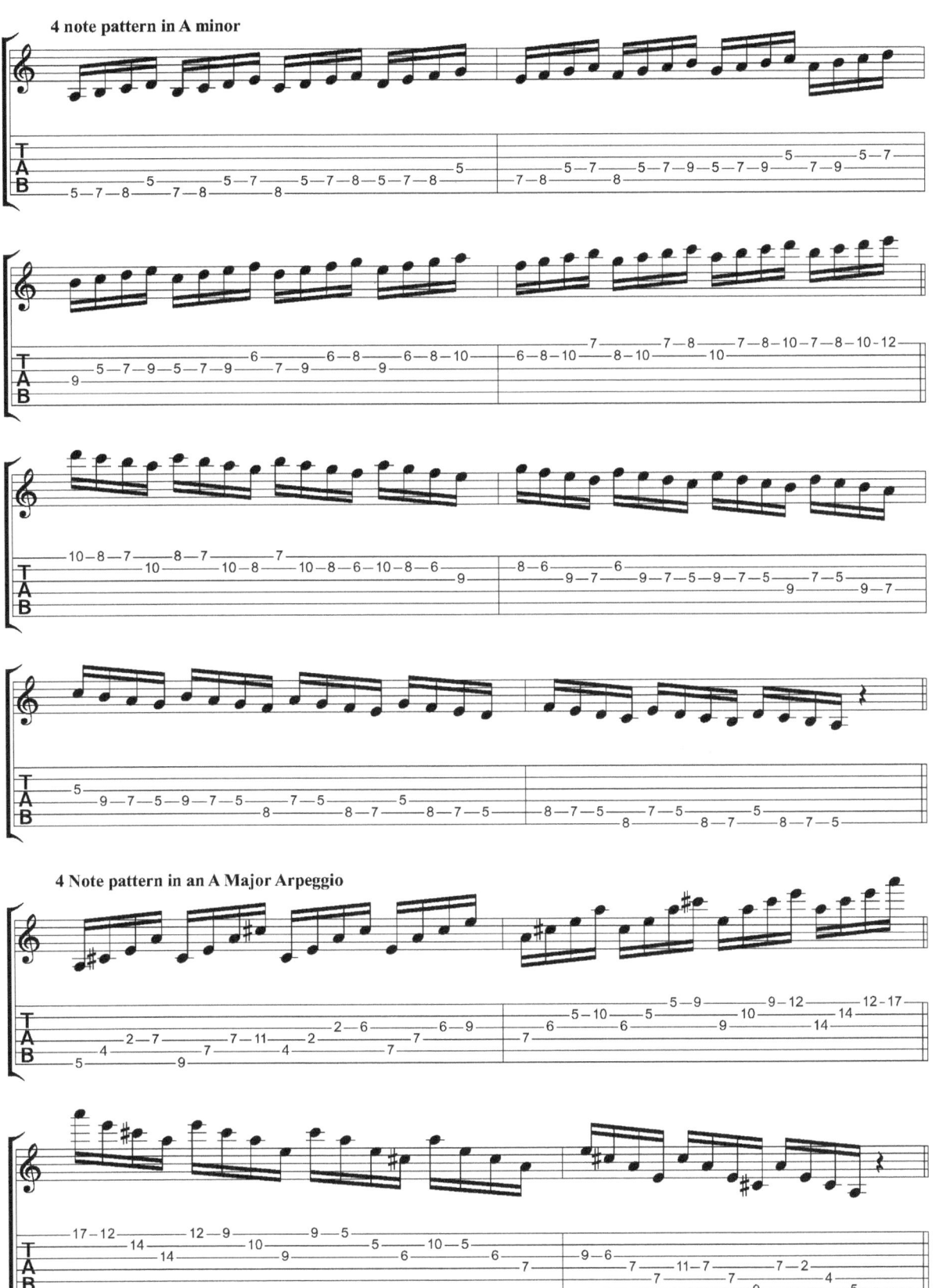

Up 2 down 1 pattern in A minor

Up 2 down 1 pattern in an A Major Arpeggio

Up 2 down 1 pattern in an A minor Arpeggio

Guitar in Theory and Practice

Rhythm

Analyze how melodies, licks and riffs relate to time. Think of the basic pulse or beat and look at how many notes are played inside each beat. It is a good exercise to divide the beat evenly into different parts. Start by hitting one note evenly over and over again. This note can be any note from the open low E to any high note played staccato or legato, with any tone, with or without distortion, and played with or without palm muting. When using a metronome, first try hitting one note directly on each click. Try this using both downstrokes and alternate picking.

Try these exercises with a metronome set at a slow to moderate tempo in 4/4.

Start with hitting one note for every beat (**Quarter Notes**).

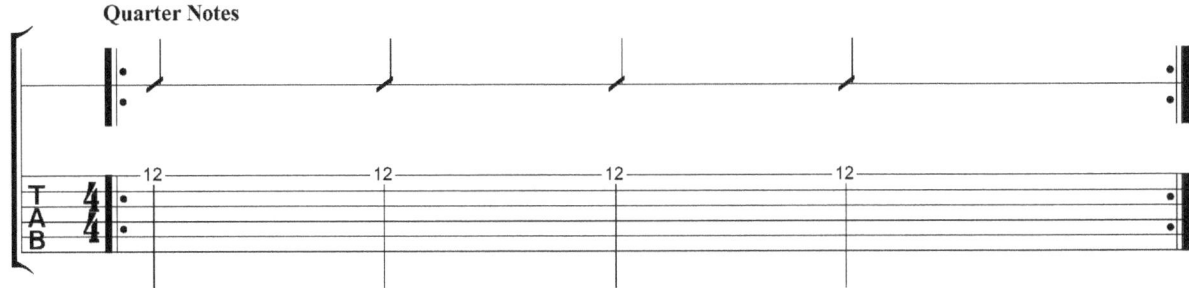

Then, try hitting two notes for every beat (**8th Notes**).

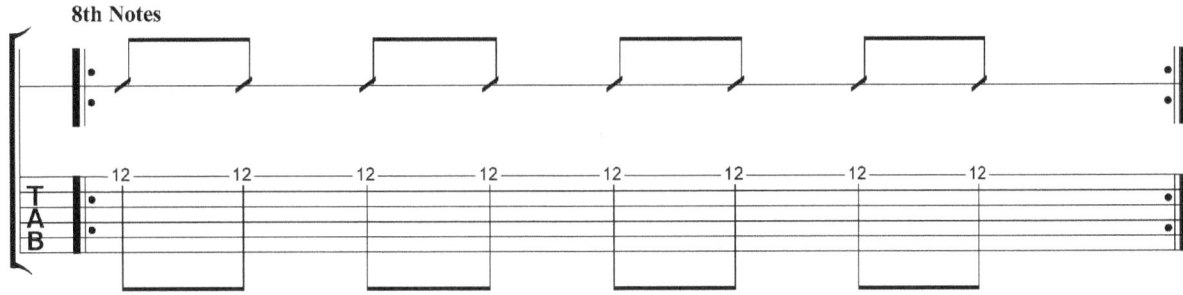

Then, try hitting four notes for every beat (**16th Notes**).

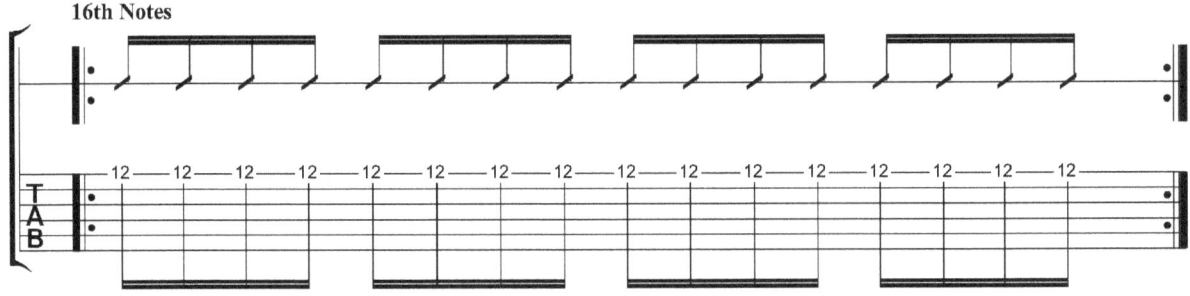

Then, try hitting three notes for every beat (**Triplets**).

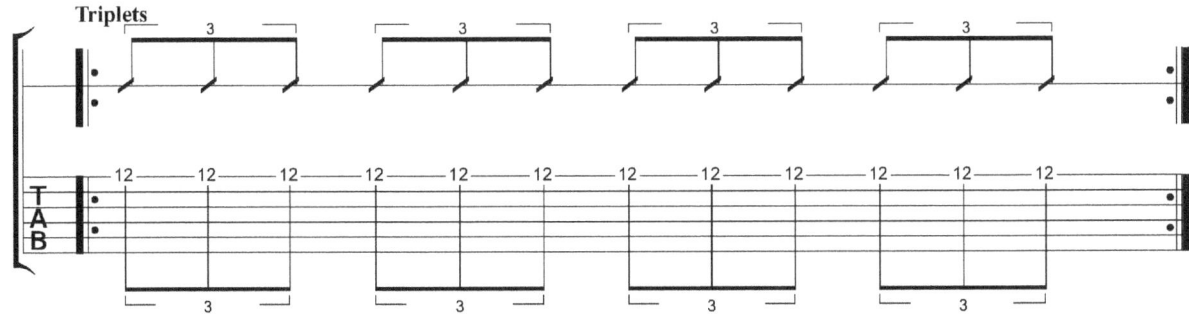

Then, try hitting six notes for every beat (**Sextuplets**).

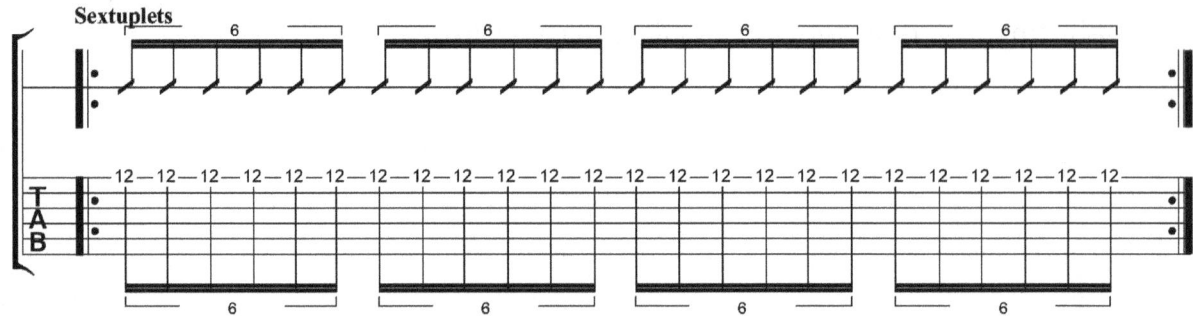

Then, try hitting eight notes for every beat (**32nd Notes**).

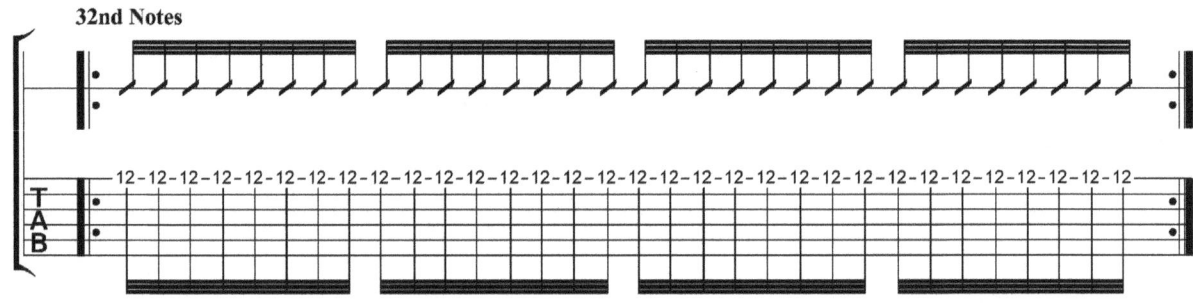

Then, try hitting five notes for every beat (**Quintuplets**).

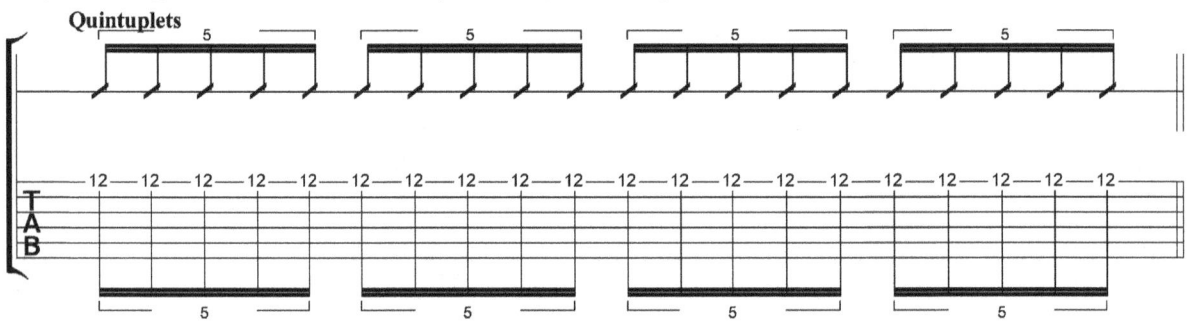

Then, try hitting seven notes for every beat (**Septuplets**).

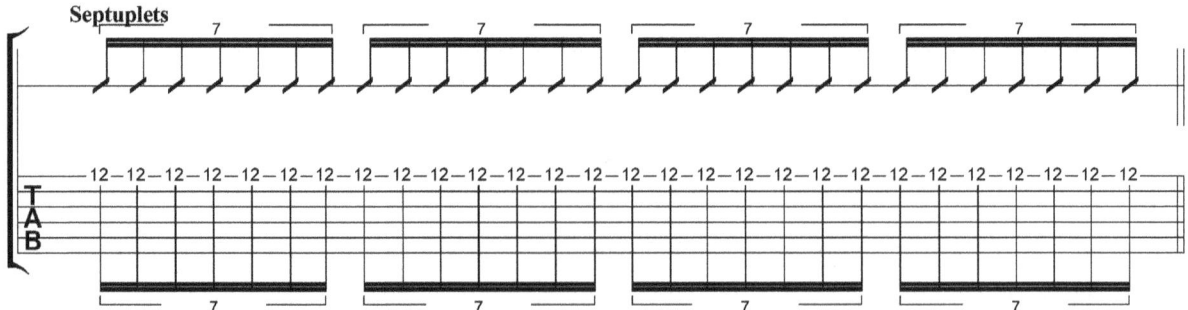

Try switching from one rhythm to another while staying in time.

Start by going from **Quarter Notes** to **8th Notes**.

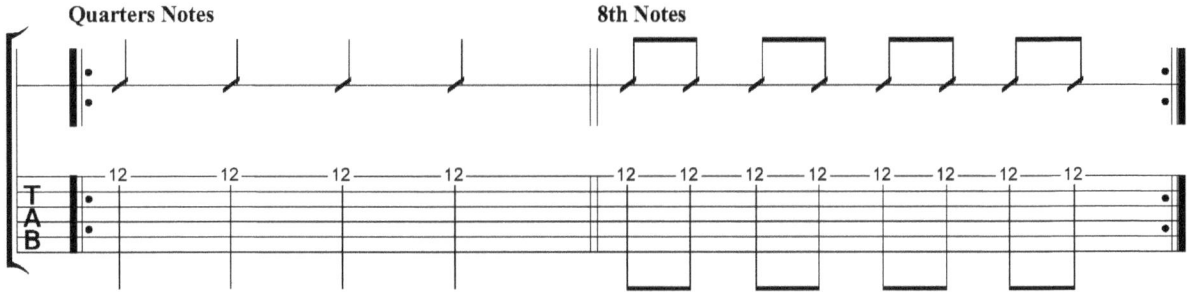

Then, try going from **Quarter Notes** to **8th Notes** to **16th Notes**.

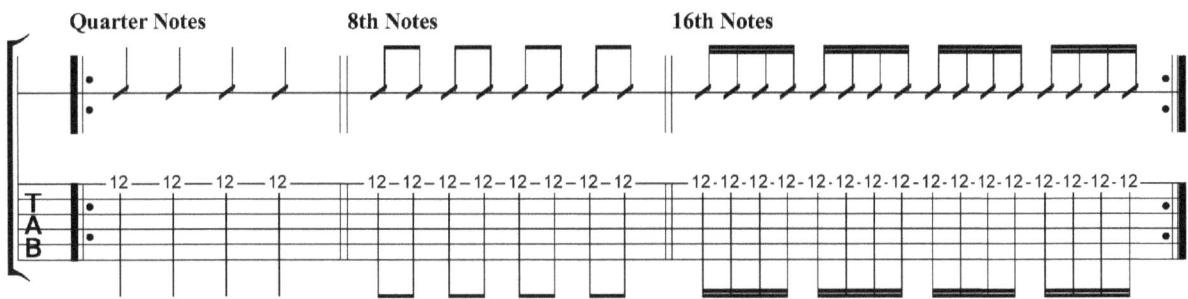

Then, try going from **Quarter Notes** to **Triplets**.

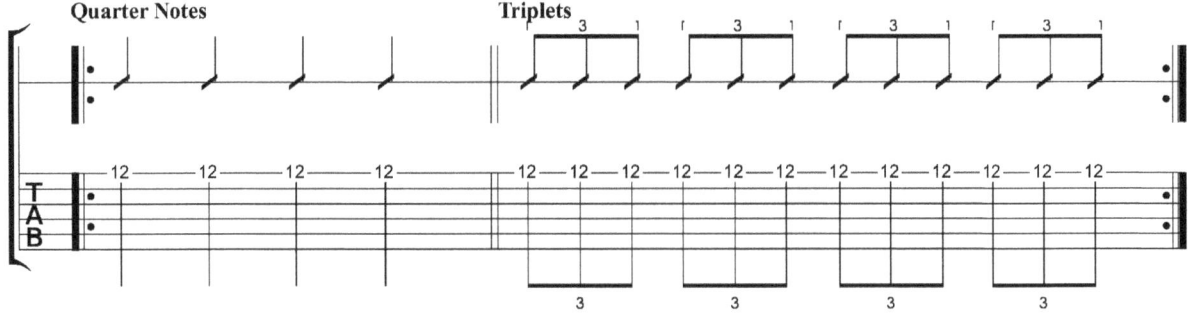

Then, try going from **Quarter Notes** to **Triplets** to **Sextuplets**.

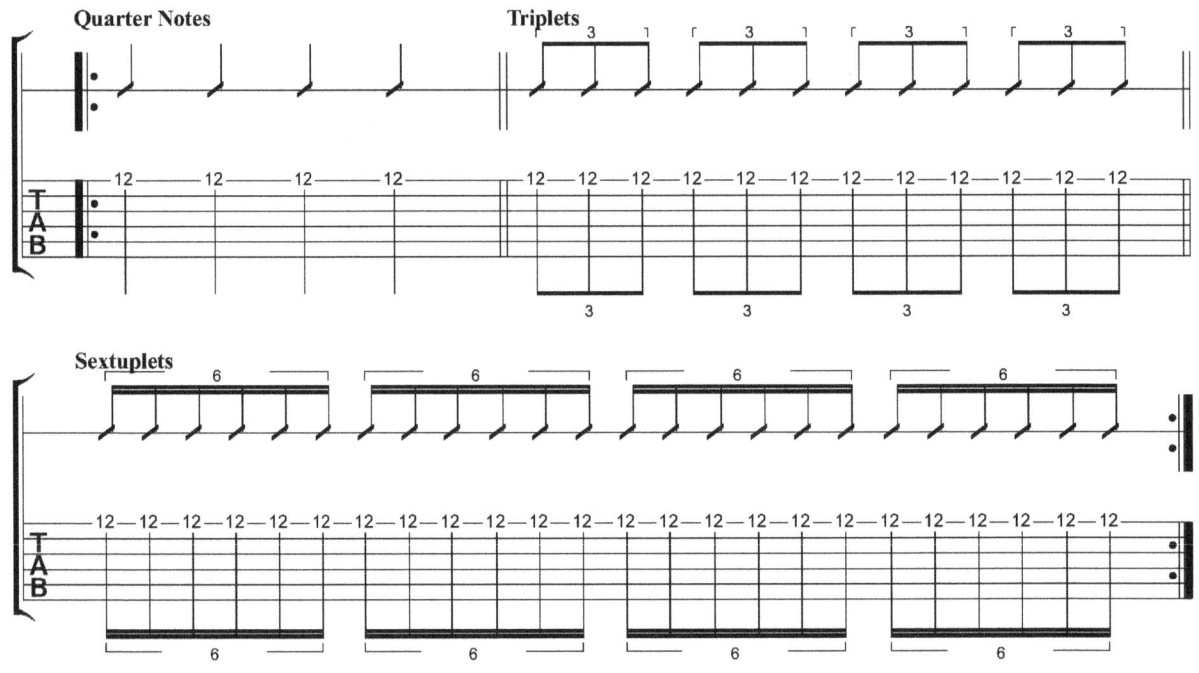

Then, try going from **Quarter Notes** to **8ths** to **Triplets** to **Sixteenths**.

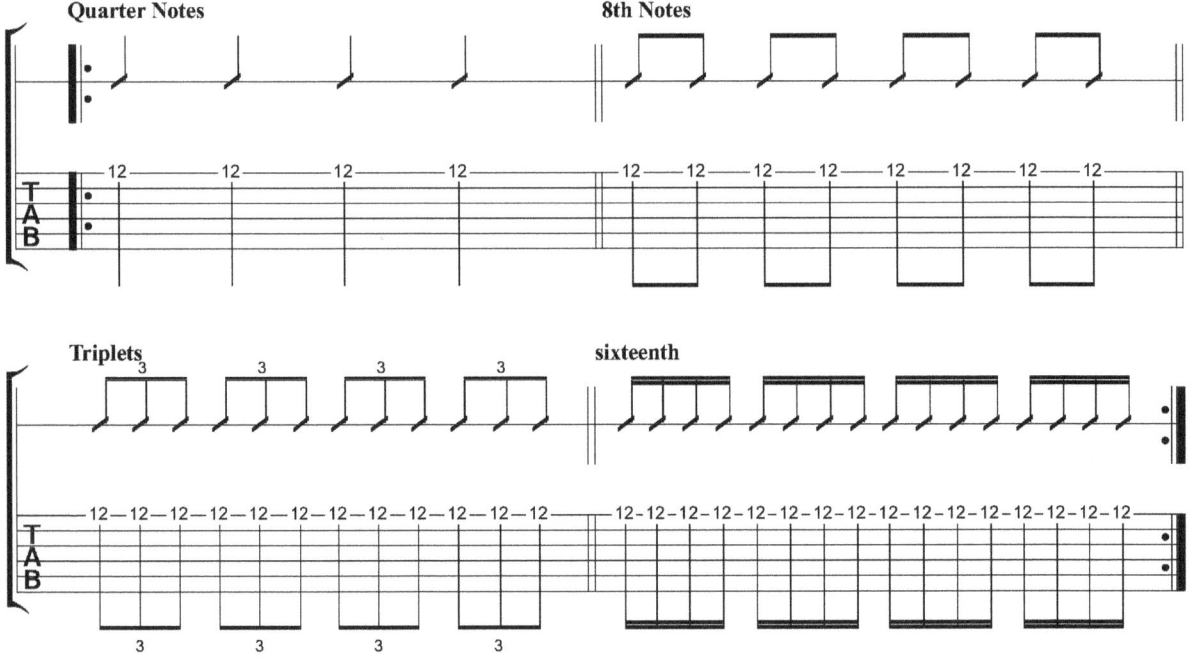

Then, try going from **Quarter Notes** to **8ths** to **Triplets** to **16ths** to **Sextuplets**.

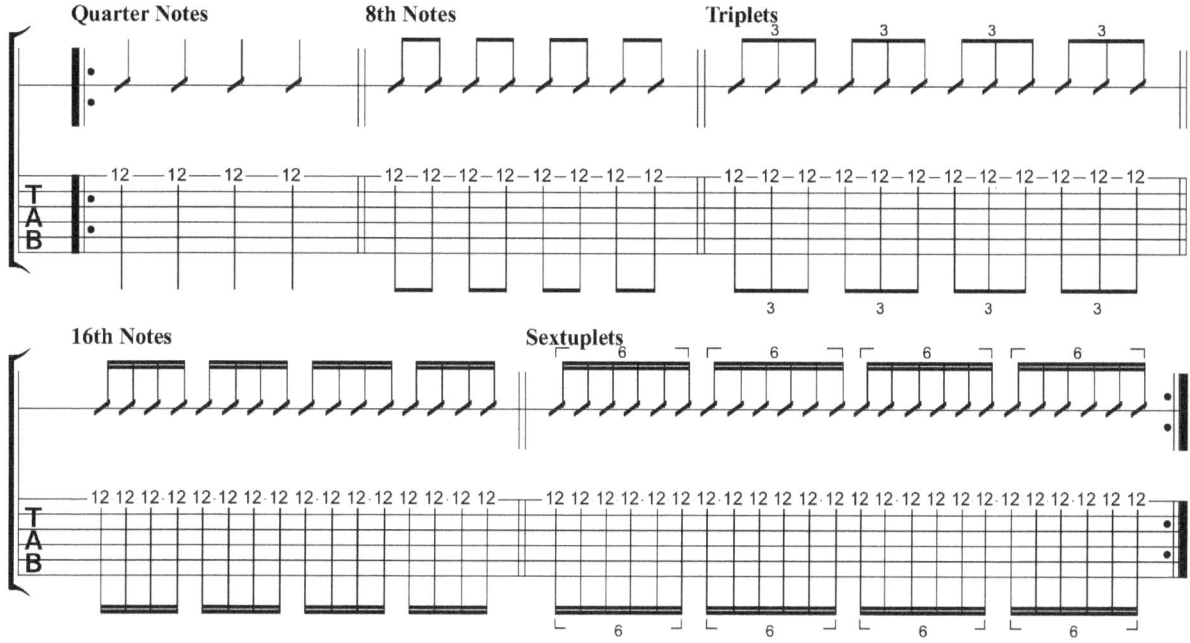

Then, try going from **Quarter Notes** to **Eighths** to **Triplets** to **16ths** to **Sextuplets** to **32nd Notes**.

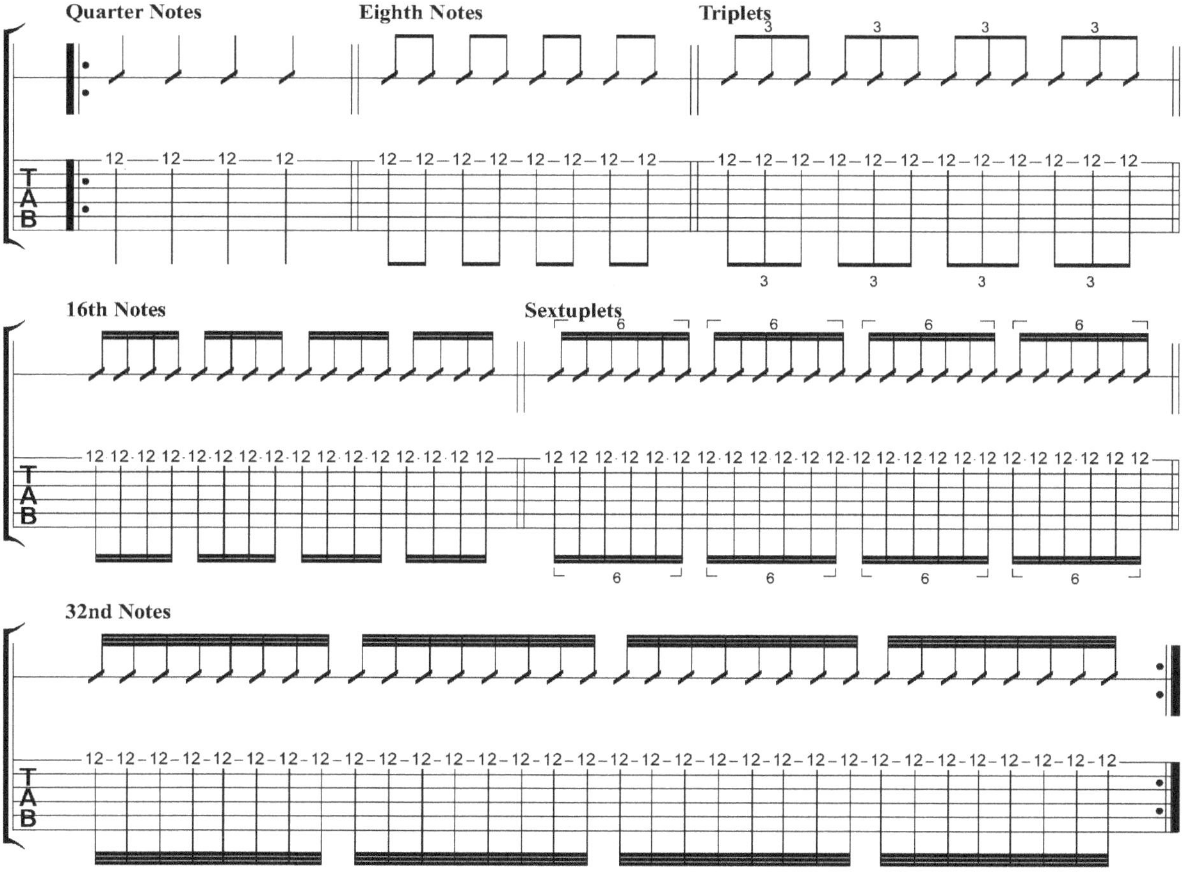

Also, work on playing just on the upbeat (reggae style).

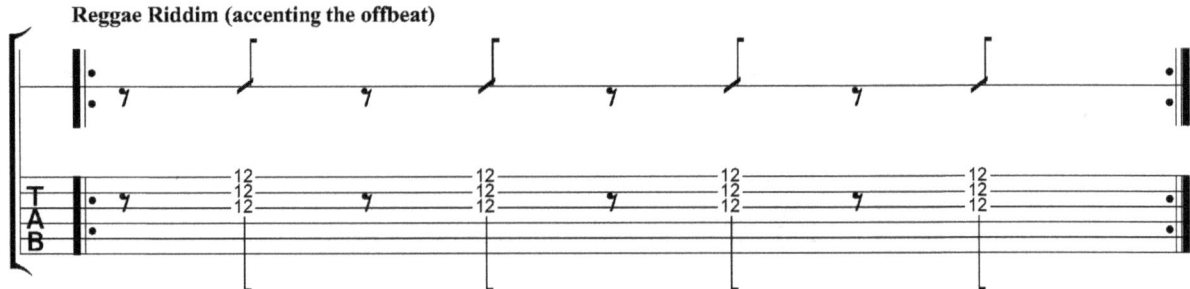

Work on syncopated **8th Note** rhythms.

Work on syncopated **16th Note** rhythms (they are good for funk using a ninth chord and metal using an E power chord.)

Also, work on **Quarter Note Triplets**. To play **Quarter Note Triplets** you would count regular **8th Note Triplets**, but hit every other one.

(*1* and *a*, *2 and* a, *3* and *a*, 4 *and* a) this gives us a way to hit three even notes for every two beats.

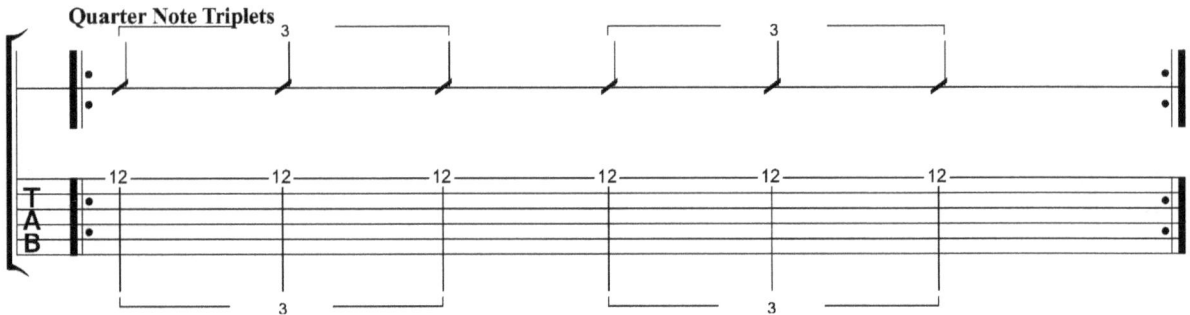

Also, try these ideas in odd time signatures.

Chord Scales (Basic Division of Triads and Seventh Chords)

I feel that if you just hit random notes within the parameters of the modes, pentatonic scales, and arpeggios, you are bound to come up with some cool ideas for solos. However, it is very important to learn how chords and scales relate to one another.

This means that you must make sure that you understand chord scales. We can put a chord on every note of the major scale. This is what a chord scale is. Each mode has a chord that works for it. The first mode is Ionian; the first chord is major, so Ionian works for a major chord. The second mode is Dorian; the second chord is minor, so Dorian works for a minor chord. Modes relate to their respected chords (similar to how each sun sign in astrology is related to a planet, element, etc.).

To be a great musician you really must study and memorize chords and scales, but learning how they relate to each other, and everything else for that matter, is of supreme importance.

Check out the poster at the end of the book for a chart/map that reveals the relationships of astrological signs, pitches, colors, intervals, planets, gods, elements, dualities, time, intervals, numbers, and chakras.

Chord Scales, Modes, Solfege and Steps
(Whole Steps and Half Steps)

Key of C Major

(Ionian is *the* major scale and Aeolian is *the* minor scale)

	I	ii	iii	IV	V	vi	vii	I
Chords	C major	D minor	E minor	F major	G major	A minor	B dim	C major
Modes	Ionian	Dorian	Phrygian	Lydian	Mixolydian	Aeolian	Locrian	Ionian
Solfege	Do	Re	Mi	Fa	So	La	Ti	Do
Steps		1	1	½	1	1	1	½

If you can memorize the chord scale, then you can figure out what key a chord progression (or riff) is in. This is how you can figure out what scale to use for a solo over a riff. In other words, it is how to figure out what scale to use for a melody line over a chord progression. You must also learn the chord scales for minor keys, harmonic minor keys and melodic minor keys. Then, try to learn the chord scales for other types of scales that you play.

Ways to Find the Keys of Chord Progressions (or Riffs) in Major Keys:

If a riff or progression has:

Two minor chords a whole step apart, then the chords are ii and iii.

Two major chords a whole step apart, then the chords are IV and V.

Two power chords a half step apart, then the chords are iii and IV.

A diminished chord is vii.

If you find out what I is, that is the major key you are in.

Here is an example:

Say the chord progression (or riff) is a C major chord to a D major chord, and you need to know what key you are in or what scale to use to solo over it.

Well, looking at the major chord scale we see that two major chords one whole step apart are IV and V in a major key. So then you would know that C major is the IV chord and D major would be the V chord. Since C is the IV chord in this example, you can play in C Lydian because Lydian is the 4th mode. You can also just figure out what I is, and then play that major scale (Ionian). So, this progression of a C major chord to a D major chord is in the key of G major. In this example you can play a G major scale, or a C Lydian scale which have the same notes.

Need another example? No problem, here you go:

Say the chord progression (or riff) is a D minor chord to an E minor chord, and you need to know what key you are in or what scale to use to solo over it.

Looking at the major chord scale we see that two minor chords one whole step apart are ii and iii in a major key. So, then you know that D minor is the ii chord and that the E minor would be the iii chord. Since D is the ii chord in this example, you can play in D Dorian because Dorian is the second mode. You can also just figure out what I is, and then play that major scale (Ionian). So, this progression of a D minor chord to an E minor chord is in the key of C major. In this example, you can play a C major scale or a D Dorian scale as these scales have the same notes.

Chord Scales in Major, Minor, Harmonic Minor, and Melodic Minor Keys

Key of A Major

I	ii	iii	IV	V	vi	vii	I
A Major	Bm	C#m7	D Major	E Major	F#m	G#dim	A Major
A Maj7	Bm7	C#m7	D Maj.7	E7	F#m7	G#½dim	A Maj7

Key of A Minor

I	ii	III	Iv	V	VI	VII	I
Am	B dim	C Major	Dm	Em	F Major	G Major	Am
Am7	B½ dim	C Maj7	Dm7	Em7	F Maj7	G7	Am7

Key of A Harmonic Minor

I	ii	III+	Iv	V	VI	vii	I
Am	B dim	C Aug	Dm	E Major	F Major	G#dim	Am
Am/Maj7	B½dim	C Maj7#5	Dm7	E7	F Maj7	G#dim.7	Am/Maj7

- **Diminished and diminished 7th chord substitutions in harmonic minor**
  Diminished 7th chords work every three frets up or down as inversions. Any note can be the root. Diminished 7th chords can be substituted for the ii, iv, VI or vii chords in harmonic minor keys. So, that means that B diminished 7th, D diminished 7th, F diminished 7th, and G#diminished 7th chords all work in A harmonic minor, as well as B diminished, D diminished, F diminished and G# diminished chords.

- **Augmented chord substitutions in harmonic minor**
  Augmented chords work every four frets up or down as inversions. Any note can be the root. Augmented chords can be substituted for the III, V, and vii chords in harmonic minor. So that means that C augmented, E augmented, and G#augmented all work in A harmonic minor.

Key of A Melodic minor

I	ii	III+	IV	V	Vi	vii	I
Am	Bm	C Aug.	D Major	E Major	F#dim	G#dim	Am
Am/Maj7	Bm7	CMaj7#5	D7	E7	F#½dim	G#½dim	Am/Maj7

Augmented chord substitutions work in melodic minor as III, V and vii.

- **Tritone substitutions in melodic minor**

    A dominant seventh chord works as the IV and V chord, but also can be used as a substitution for the vii chord if the 5th is altered or omitted. By lowering the 5th and the 9th of the V or vii chords in a melodic minor key, we end up with the same chord. That means they are bitonal. So a G#7♭9♭5 chord is the same as a D♭9♭5 chord. This is known as a tritone substitution.

    D7, E7, and G#7(no 5th) all work in A melodic minor.

Formulas for Chords, Arpeggios and Scales

Chords/Triads
Major (1, 3, 5)

Minor (1, ♭3, 5)

Diminished (1, ♭3, ♭5)

Augmented (1, 3, ♯5)

Diatonic Seventh Chords
Major 7th (1, 3, 5, 7)

Minor 7th (1, ♭3, 5, ♭7)

Dominant 7th (1, 3, 5, ♭7)

½ Diminished (1, ♭3, ♭5, ♭7)

Major/Minor 7th (1, ♭3, 5, ♭7)

Major 7♯5 (1, 3, ♯5, 7)

Pentatonic Scales
Major Pentatonic Scale (1, 2, 3, 5, 6)

Minor Pentatonic Scale (1, ♭3, 4, 5, ♭7)

Blues Scales
Major Blues Scale (1, 2, ♭3, 3, 5, 6)

Minor Blues Scale (1, ♭3, 4, ♭5, 5, ♭7)

Modes in Major Keys

Ionian (1, 2, 3, 4, 5, 6, 7)

Dorian (1, 2, ♭3, 4, 5, 6, ♭7)

Phrygian (1, ♭2, ♭3, 4, 5, ♭6, ♭7)

Lydian (1, 2, 3, ♯4, 5, 6, 7)

Mixolydian (1, 2, 3, 4, 5, 6, ♭7)

Aeolian (1, 2, ♭3, 4, 5, ♭6, ♭7)

Locrian (1, ♭2, ♭3, 4, ♭5, ♭6, ♭7)

Modes in Minor Keys

Aeolian (1, 2, ♭3, 4, 5, ♭6, ♭7)

Locrian (1, ♭2, ♭3, 4, ♭5, ♭6, ♭7)

Ionian (1, 2, 3, 4, 5, 6, 7)

Dorian (1, 2, ♭3, 4, 5, 6, ♭7)

Phrygian (1, ♭2, ♭3, 4, 5, ♭6, ♭7)

Lydian (1, 2, 3, ♯4, 5, 6, 7)

Mixolydian (1, 2, 3, 4, 5, 6, ♭7)

Modes in Harmonic Minor Keys

Harmonic Minor Scale (1, 2, ♭3, 4, 5, ♭6, 7)

2nd Mode in Harm. Minor Locrian Natural 6 (1, ♭2, ♭3, 4, ♭5, 6, ♭7)

Ionian ♯5 (1, 2, 3, 4, ♯5, 6, 7)

Dorian ♯4 (1, 2, ♭3, ♯4, 5, 6, ♭7)

Phrygian Dominant (1, ♭2, 3, 4, 5, ♭6, ♭7)

6th Mode in Harmonic Minor Lydian w/♯2 (1, ♯2, 3, ♯4, 5, 6, 7)

7th Mode of Harmonic Minor (1, ♭2, ♭3, ♭4, ♭5, ♭6, ♭♭7)

Modes in Melodic Minor Keys

Melodic Minor Scale (1, 2, ♭3, 4, 5, 6, 7)

Dorian ♭2 (1, ♭2, ♭3, 4, 5, 6, ♭7)

3rd Mode of Melodic Minor (1, 2, 3, ♯4, ♯5, 6, 7)

Lydian Dominant (1, 2, 3, ♯4, 5, 6, ♭7)

5th Mode of Melodic Minor Mixolydian w/ ♭6 (1, 2, 3, 4, 5, ♭6, ♭7)

Aeolian ♭5 (1, 2, ♭3, 4, ♭5, ♭6, ♭7)

Super Locrian (1, ♭2, ♭3, ♭4, ♭5, ♭6, ♭7)

Transcendental Wisdom

Where and When to Practice

I recommend practicing in different rooms of the house and at different times of the day. Some may find that the more practical memorizing type of work is better done in the morning, and the more creative work is better done at night. While others, especially many rock, blues, country and metal players that I know, find that they cannot do anything very well in the morning.

Metaphysical Secret about Guitars

All organisms vibrate to a certain frequency. For thousands of years many Pagans, Christians, drugged-out hippies, and touched people of all kinds have claimed that they can see the color of auras surrounding trees and other organisms. Many new age, magick and occult books speak of this, as well.

Whether you believe in this or not, the fact of the matter is that the wood from the body and/or neck of a guitar vibrates at a certain frequency. The indefinite pitch of the sound of you hitting or tapping the body and/or neck of your guitar with your knuckle is actually a pitch. This pitch should not be a 7th, $\flat 5^{th}$ or a $\flat 2^{nd}$ above or below the key you want to play in. If it is, you should consider tuning that guitar down a half step. This is why it may feel subliminally as if some guitars resonate better in certain keys. Resonance is an ancient magical secret.

Steve Vai, in a 2010 interview with *Guitar World*, essentially stated that if the neck and body are not in harmony with each other, then the guitar will resonate poorly.

It is worth the time to figure out which keys your guitars will play best in for resonance, sustain, and tone. Hopefully, you got lucky and have a guitar that vibrates to an E, since we are always playing in E so damn much.

Unlimited Perspectives

I think it is foolish to limit ourselves to any one specific genre of music, even if we primarily only play one specific genre of music. We must look at music as sounds with different rhythms. We must learn to understand how sounds relate to other sounds. Exploring concepts from all styles of music is important in gaining the knowledge to become adept at whatever style we may play primarily. We should also study the music from other instruments to broaden the spectrum of possibilities.

I also stress the importance of having different perspectives on the same things. It is important to understand something in more than one way in order to gain new insights and the ability to approach things in different ways. For instance, a major scale can be thought of as a scale. However, we may come up with new ideas if we think of it also as a pentatonic scale with two additional notes, or as a major triad with four additional notes, or as a chromatic scale missing five of the notes, etc.

The Magick of Musick

When learning a scale or chord, it is important to memorize the name and fingering. It is also important to learn how to improvise with it and to make it sound like music that you enjoy. It is then very important to have a personal relationship with each chord and scale in order to understand the ultimate feeling it evokes in the listener. This will also teach us the art of text painting for when we need to put music to words, or words to music.

I find that musick (yeah, I do spell it with a k at the end sometimes), like all of the arts, is a reflection of life. The musick that we write, and even the solos and melodies we play, are always directly correlated to our personalities and our lives. If we can become the person that we want to be, then we can become the player that we want to be. If we can become the player that we want to be, we can become the person that we want to be. If we can develop our personalities, we can become better artists, allowing us to augment the state of mankind as a whole.

The magick comes in to play when we understand the feelings that the various sounds evoke in the listeners and ourselves. This allows us to have the power to change the listener's thoughts at will. We must also always try to understand how musick (and art) relates to all things. Don't go insane, but check out the poster that relates astrological signs, pitches, colors, intervals, planets, gods, elements, dualities, time, intervals numbers, and chakras. This is not a new idea, and I became aware of all of these things by reading Pythagoras and understanding the music of the spheres. The colors of the rainbow follow the seven note names. This is a common idea found in several magick books I read when I was a troubled teenager. Uli Jon Roth once told me that he had figured out the relationships of time to the musical intervals. It made perfect sense after he explained it to me, especially seeing that a ♭5 is midnight.

Dwelling on this knowledge really helps us understand our personality in relation to musick so we can gain individuality in our playing and lives. This also allows us to gain insight into the relationships of all things.

Be Yourself

Although learning to play like your favorite musicians is very important at first, it is also important to learn to play like your least favorite musicians as well. Why? Well, if they suck so much then it should be super easy to play like them, right? OK.

Think about why theoretically you like some music styles more than others. You must discover *your sound* and not just be a copy of various musicians that you like.

Make sure you are playing music for the right reasons. You should play music because you love music, not to get money or chicks, or to try to be cool, or any other impure reasons. We must try to live a life that will allow us to be the best guitarist that we can be. Don't smoke crack (or shoot heroin). If you do, the odds are good that you will lose your talent and probably die or end up in jail. Unfortunately, the rewards for musicians are money, sex, drugs and alcohol. These so called rewards are also the biggest pitfalls. They can easily take away your talent, as well as rob you of your livelihood. Also, if you are playing to try to get respect from others, then you are probably just trying to feed your ego.

If we are too self conscious, scared or shy, we cannot express our emotions wholly to play at our best. Some are insecure because they are scared of the judgment of others. This can prevent them from ever developing into the player that they could be. Please do not let this happen to you. Sometimes it takes a lot of strength to go out there and make a bold statement with art, especially under hostile conditions. It can be humiliating to try to express yourself artistically. Conversely, it can also feel as if eternal light is showering upon your soul when you do it right. Unfortunately, I think for many it feels both ways. This is why we must constantly work on our personalities and be strong. Remember, our personality is directly related to our playing. Be bold to evolve the state of musick for future generations.

I hope some of this info has helped you to become better. Share this information with the uninitiated. Please check out www.kevinmbuck.com to sample or purchase my musick or to contact me.

Extras

Extras

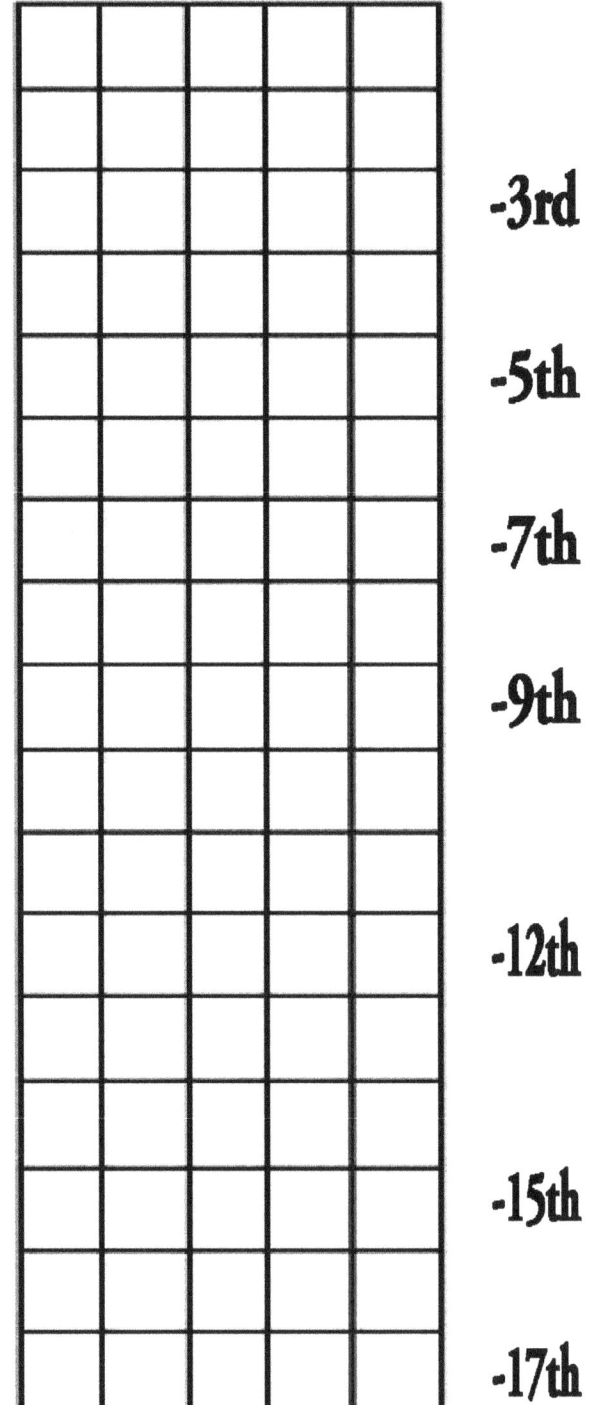

Extras

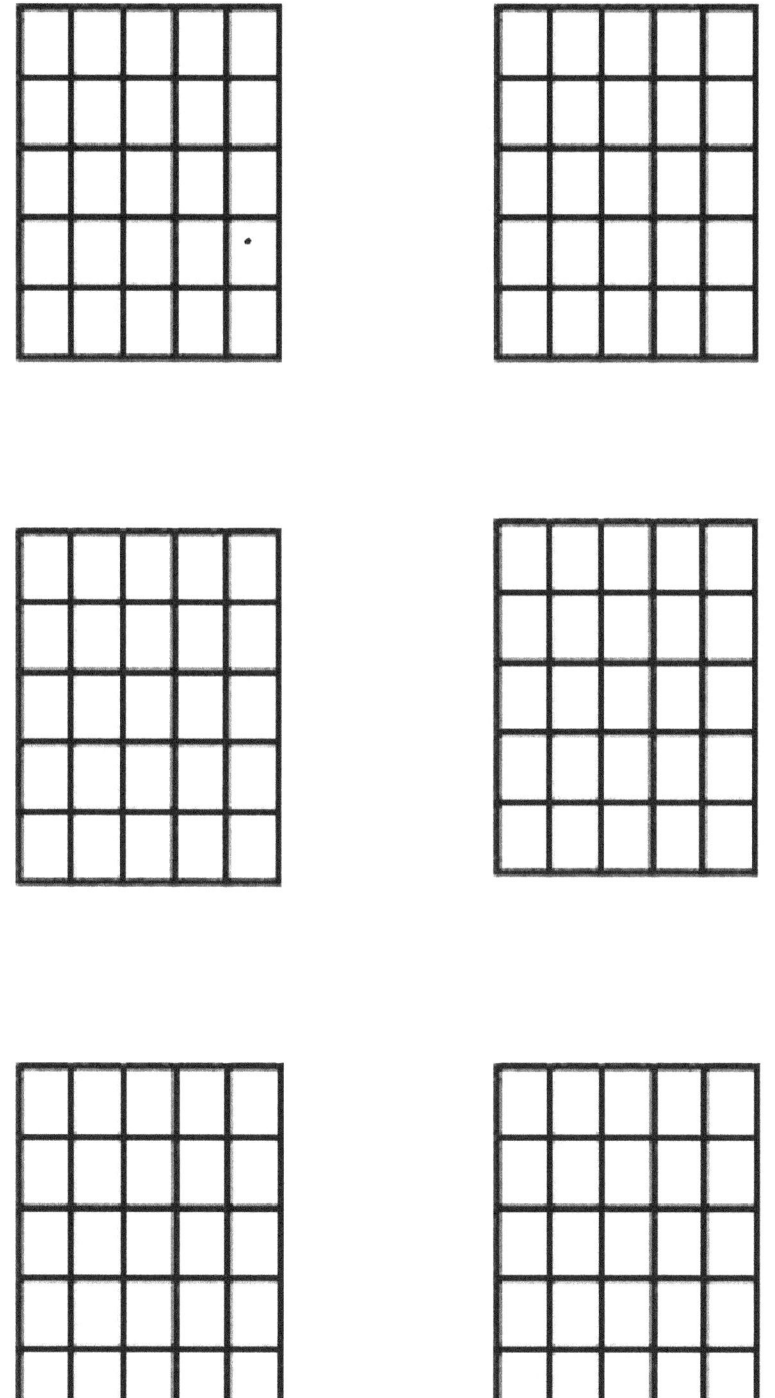

Extras

	Aries	Taurus	Gemini	Cancer	Leo	Virgo	Libra	Scorpio	Sagittarius	Capricorn	Aquarius	Pisces
Pitch	A	A#/Bb	B	C	C#/Db	D	D#/Eb	E	F	F#/Gb	G	G#/Ab
Color	Red	Orange		Yellow		Green		Blue	Indigo		Violet	
Planet	Mars	Venus	Mercury	Moon	Sun	Mercury	Venus	Pluto	Jupiter	Saturn	Uranus	Neptune
God	Ares	Aphrodite	Hermes	Selene	Apollo	Hecamede	Aphrodite	Hades	Zeus	Cronus	Uranus	Poseidon
Element	Fire	Earth	Air	Water	Fire	Earth	Air	Water	Fire	Earth	Air	Water
Duality	Male ♂	Female ♀	Male ♂	Female ♀	Male ♂	Female ♀	Male ♂	Female ♀	Male ♂	Female ♀	Male ♂	Female ♀
Time	Noon	2 PM	4 PM	6 PM	8 PM	10 PM	Midnight	2 AM	4 AM	6 AM	8 AM	10 AM
Interval	unison	b2	2	b3	3	4	b5	5	b6	6	b7	7
Number	1	2	3	4	5	6	7	8	9	10	11	12
Mode	Ionian	Dorian		Phrygian		Lydian		Mixolydian	Aeolian		Locrian	
Chakra	Root	Sacrum		Solar Plexus		Heart		Throat	3rd Eye		Crown	

Extras   *Guitar in Theory and Practice*

www.ingramcontent.com/pod-product-compliance
Lightning Source LLC
Chambersburg PA
CBHW080521110426
42742CB00017B/3196